'MIM'

Dame Marie Rambert, DBE, in later years.

'MIM'
A PERSONAL MEMOIR OF MARIE RAMBERT

Brigitte Kelly

Dance Books • Alton

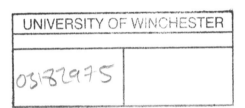
First published 2009
Dance Books Ltd, The Old Bakery,
4 Lenten Street, Alton, Hampshire GU34 1HG

ISBN 978 1 85273 127 4

A CIP catalogue record for this title
is available from the British Library

Printed in Great Britain by Latimer Trend and Company Ltd,
Plymouth, Devon

CONTENTS

To my Mother

Acknowledgements

For their generous help in the writing and production of this book I would like to express my thanks to Christopher Bruce, Thérèse Cantine, Helen (Lulu) Dukes, Angela (Dukes) Ellis, David Ellis, Robert Harrold, Jackie Hinden, Jonathan Hinden, David Leonard, Norman Morrice, James Palmer, Jane Pritchard, Elisabeth Schooling, Josephine Turnbull, Hans-Theodor Wohlfahrt.

Brigitte Kelly

Foreword by Christopher Bruce, CBE

It was with enormous pleasure that I read through a draft of Brigitte Kelly's account of Marie Rambert's life and work; for these pages vividly brought to life this tenacious midwife of British ballet and the settings where the magical process of dance-making took place. It was an emotional read, reminding me once again of all that was achieved from such humble beginnings and within an environment where her early efforts were never given the support – or the burden – of being institutionalised. The company was born out of and continues to exist in what Marie Rambert called, her 'blessed poverty'.

Stirring so many memories, Brigitte's down to earth and affectionate memoir helped me better understand my own history. I was again reminded – if indeed I ever needed to be – of what a remarkable and complex woman Rambert was. Her great achievements were attained almost in spite of herself. Of course, she had remarkable artistic vision and an uncanny instinct for spotting talent and, where talent was limited, the ability to push artists to succeed beyond expectations. But, as Brigitte quite rightly states, Marie Rambert had never been a dancer of any standing, her ballet teaching was technically suspect and, particularly in the early days, she was considered an amateur by many in the profession. Her behaviour, especially towards her dancers, could be appalling, sometimes psychologically damaging. She had no head for business and was totally impractical. However, everything Rambert engaged in was done with wholehearted passion and energy. She was a wonderful coach and, as a young member of her company, I enjoyed the somewhat masochistic pleasure of solo rehearsals with her, knowing that the experience was a rare one and instinctively sensing that it would bear fruit. She instilled in me a belief that I could achieve anything I wanted as long as I was prepared to work for it and make the necessary sacrifices. In retrospect, I realise how powerfully her beliefs were handed on to those who crossed her path and have become second nature to many of us.

I enjoyed Brigitte's descriptions of the colourful personalities who feature in the history of the school and company, about some of whom I have vivid memories. However, I was a relative latecomer, joining the school in 1959. The amenities, as Brigitte describes, were fairly basic. I remember the overcrowded boy's dressing room equipped with just one shower; the smell, the heat and the conversations between an assorted group of boys from extraordinarily diverse backgrounds. I recall the excitement generated when professional dancers turned up to participate in school classes. Despite the inadequacies of the building and, at times, some idiosyncratic teaching methods, I believe these artists were, in part, drawn to the Mercury Theatre because they understood its place in history. Here, born out the influences of Diaghilev's Ballets Russes, a unique tradition was formed, one that has affected dance throughout the world.

Reading Brigitte's memories of the company's early work – what I would describe as intimate chamber ballets and the uniquely expressive artists who danced them – I was struck by the idea that these are the very qualities that, to this day, remain the hallmarks of the company.

Alongside many others, I feel so privileged to have been part of the Rambert story. I am both happy and grateful that Brigitte Kelly has put her memories to paper. It is a story which deals with both the private person and the pioneering artist. It is a most valuable account of one of the most extraordinary and important personalities of 20th century dance.

INTRODUCTION

'You knew her as well as anybody', her daughter Angela said when she asked me to write about Mim. She was more than simply my dance teacher, she moulded my thinking, challenged my intelligence; she was a kind of balletic mother figure. She and my mother were the greatest influences in my life and they were friends right up to my mother's death in 1952.

There were several women in Marie Rambert. We all show different images of ourselves to different people and no one did that more than Rambert. She was part inspired amateur and part tough professional, proud of her company, graciously taking centre stage for her *révérence* alongside her dancers then hurling abuse at them the moment the curtain dropped. Perhaps the real woman revealed herself in her teaching? Maybe there in the classroom she was truly herself, so passionately involved that she dropped the other masks and in doing so often lost control of her tongue.

But then what about the other woman who came to my wedding reception and the room being crowded shared an armchair with my husband's Polish aunt Marie-Louise when they chattered away like a couple of typical grannies? There was the ingratiating, almost servile attitude to the great and powerful; the delightful, witty dinner party guest; the self-promoting, pushy Jewish personality. They were a marvellous series of acts and she was often deliberately outrageous, wanting to be quoted, demanding attention by turning cartwheels if all else failed.

Inside was another shrewd, perceptive person, looking, watching, calculating, assessing, ridiculing, a curiously insensitive person in the way only self-obsessed people can be. She never meant harm and apologised not once but many, many times for the cruel things she may have said. 'Not for what I have done but for what I left undone', is written into the confessional prayer. She could have added, 'because my mind was focused on something else. I didn't mean to wound, I simply didn't notice.'

And there was that other earlier woman, the East European woman, warm, almost archaic. Her parsimony was interpreted as meanness by people from the rich Western world. Her belief in folklore, superstitions, the atavistic ritual, was derived from an ancient eastern culture.

And there was in old age the matriarch sitting upright on the sofa, or walking alone in Holland Park, her feet remembering the soil of Poland. She had a mania for economy, eternally turning off lights, hating waste, reminding herself of her spartan upbringing in her native land where she had everything she needed – only there wasn't that much to be had.

So many people in one person – how could anyone know her wholly? Perhaps it was after all the dancers who got the real woman, the kernel of this turbulent, tough little nut. If she had been a foot taller and less foreign she would have found more dignity in her earlier life, instead of only acquiring it in old age. No wonder one of her most repeated instructions to her dancers was to 'look up and corners of the mouth up' – that could have been her epitaph.

CHAPTER 1

In the liberated Poland of the late 90s I trudged up the hill to the old city of Warsaw and sat in the *Stare Miasto*, the main square, basking in the summer sun. Old City – not exactly. The cleverly recreated façades constructed from old photographs like film sets were no doubt accurate, picturesque certainly, but there was something missing. Ghosts haunted the narrow streets crammed with tourists meandering over the buried bones and rubble of the ancient city.

In my imagination I pictured Warsaw as it must have been at the turn of the century when ten-year-old Cyvia Rambam (usually know as Myriam) walked purposefully to school; a background of church bells answering each other on different notes, swinging signs of saints' faces, figures of animals over inns and shops, sculptured ornamentation and cornices, secret churches and monasteries tucked away down narrow cobbled streets.

She would be dressed in her regulation dark school dress and black button boots, her black hair severely pulled back from a high forehead and an onlooker might have been struck by the mischievous intelligence in the large black eyes staring resolutely out at the world. The leather satchel would have been firmly strapped to her back but there would have been no sign of the large ornate hat that she holds in the famous photograph of 1898. Perhaps she accompanied other little girls chattering noisily like quarrelling birds. Myriam would surely have been the most vociferous and would perhaps have made her companions dissolve into giggles by suddenly performing some outlandish prank – although she was not yet performing cartwheels.

It was a cruel fate to be Polish in the late 1800s. The Poles were officially Russian subjects, but revolt was always brewing and there was a constant atmosphere of conspiracy. You had to control your tongue and not speak Polish in public places, the schools were run by spying principals who engendered profound antagonism in both teachers and pupils. The inspectors wore fine uniforms, yellow pantaloons and blue high-necked tunics with shiny brass buttons.

Myriam's school was more liberal than most thanks to Dimitri Yankovsky, a sympathetic headmaster whom Myriam loved. Polish, Jewish,

Russian and German girls sat side by side without serious disagreement. However, the pupils had to be on their guard and curb their tongues – something not easy for Myriam. She constantly overheard snatches of whispered conversation at home and in the street. Words such as 'Police', 'The Tsar', 'Deportation', 'Siberia', floated in the air. Most other children had difficulties with the Russian language, which took precedence over Polish, and some suffered despair when in spite of every effort they did not understand the lessons. This was not so with Myriam. Her memory was such that she could faultlessly recite a poem where her companions still struggled with the complexities of the letters. As soon as school was over each child returned to her own language, her patriotism and her religion in the safety of her home. Once a week Myriam attended a dancing class, a cursory affair which, as well as folk dancing, entailed doing classical barre exercises using each other as support and then wafting around being leaves or trees. Since Myriam loved movement she enjoyed it well enough but was not sufficiently impressed to have any desire at that time to become a ballet dancer. In fact she preferred gymnastics where she could show off her speed and verve with bravado to the other less agile children.

Her mother was Russian, father Polish, and both Jewish. Myriam had the unenviable position of being the fourth girl child, not good news, particularly in a Jewish family. The birth of twins, one of them a boy, and then another boy, resulted in Myriam being pushed aside. No one had any time for her. 'Mim' as she was called, did not have an easy relationship with her mother. Judging from old photographs this lady presents a hard, rather frightening image. Her lively little daughter was only a one-year-old when the twins arrived. In Rambert's autobiography she relates that she was never kissed or cuddled or shown much kindness. Oddly enough she hardly mentions her father and she seems to have turned to their servants for affection. These hard-working peasants whose living conditions were appalling and who received a pittance probably gave her the warmth that seems to have been lacking in her parents. It is hard to imagine that such a demonstrative, lively little girl, so full of fun, was unlovable. But she may have been a tiresome child, difficult to correct, vociferous in her demands for the attention she craved, and staging dramatic tantrums.

Although Rambert in her autobiography *Quicksilver* describes her parents' occupation as booksellers, her father was also a merchant. In spite of the Polish hatred of Tsar Nicholas II it was a time of comparative prosperity and freedom for the Jewish population, particularly if they were members of the intelligentsia. The Rambams may have been selective in their adherence to the orthodox Jewish faith. Rambert, who became a Roman Catholic when she settled in England, was troubled in old age by the dichotomy of the two religions.

I think that with Rambert the head and the heart, although not exactly in conflict, competed with each other all of her life. Her parents were intellectuals, exceptionally well read, and the contents of their bookshelves provided a rich cornucopia of literature not normally available to the average child. This foundation in literature helped her in her studies at school. Thanks to the encouragement of Yankovsky she not only read the great Polish and Russian masterpieces but also with the benefit of French taught at her school she read Corneille, Racine, Victor Hugo. Once she had settled in England, much to the astonishment of her friends, she could recite long passages of Shakespeare in accented but perfect English.

Whereas literature, art and music ranked high with the Polish middle classes, dancing was mostly associated with the peasantry who possessed an exceptionally rich culture of regional music, dances and costumes, a love of which remained with Rambert all her life. The Oberek, the fascinating and complicated Mazurka and the grand Polonaise were adapted for the ballrooms of high society. Young women of educated families were also expected to learn the social dances of the day, the Lancers, the Polka, the Waltz, as did their counterparts in Western Europe at the turn of the century.

Even though ballet was not an important part of Polish culture, in the late 1800s there would have been guest appearances from Italian and Russian ballerinas, and ballet evenings at the Warsaw Opera House where the artistic standard was poor. It is not surprising that when Rambert on her tenth birthday was taken to a performance of *Swan Lake* she was not impressed, and no doubt typically said so in no uncertain way. It was only much later, probably when she saw the Diaghilev company, that she realised how expressive classical ballet can be in the hands of a master choreographer. Until then I suspect that she merely looked upon it as a series of boring, repetitive exercises that frustrated her desire for freer, unbridled movement.

Rambert loved the country and some of her happiest moments as a child were the times when she could run wild through the fields and forest, leaping high in the air and perhaps flinging up her head and arms in an unrestrained ecstasy of freedom that was so characteristic of her nature. On fête days the Jewish village orchestra installed themselves on a platform and wrung from their fiddles intoxicating tunes and irresistible rhythms, casting such a spell on the revellers, young and old, that they danced until they dropped to the ground with exhaustion.

Never a choreographer in the real sense, Rambert from an early age invented 'free' dances for herself and, not a shy child, loved to perform them for her family and friends sometimes preluding them with a poem. When she was sixteen she saw Isadora Duncan and the experience was a vindication of her own vision of dance. No wonder that on a later occasion she tore through the barrier of the stage door to throw herself at the feet of a woman she always considered a genius. One wonders what Isadora must have made of this pushy young woman displaying a passion that even she, Isadora, with her own commitment to free dance, would have found embarrassing.

Myriam Rambam's school record was brilliant with one exception – her undisciplined behaviour. This precluded her receiving the gold medal that should have crowned her years at the Gymnasium. Not only was she troublesome in her classes but, far more seriously, in her last years of school she became increasingly involved in student unrest under the restrictive regime imposed by the new young Tsar Nicholas II.

The Poles throughout their tragic political history have always involved themselves in rebellion and protest, it is the motivating force of their lives. One of the most unhappy results of political constraint is the spontaneous ferocity it produces, particularly amongst the hot-blooded young. Rambert had grown up in an atmosphere of constant political unrest. There was always talk of liberalism, meetings were held, discussions raged in word and print about reform. There were 'Flying Universities' – teachers giving unofficial instruction to hundreds of students – conspiracies, illegal press, the smuggling of books. All of this inflamed the turbulent spirit of Rambert. She wanted to join in, she had the nature of the revolutionary and she would always need a focus for her intelligence and energy. She acted as courier, distributing illegal newspapers and propaganda leaflets under cover of dark – a risky business for if caught she would probably have ended up in Siberia or most certainly in prison. She attended clandestine meetings and, given her facility in speaking, would have given eloquent voice to her ideas. She was a loose cannon likely to explode in any direction.

Her parents became alarmed. Being Jewish, the last thing they wanted was to attract the attention of the authorities. Their daughter was uncontrolled, indiscreet, liable in a fit of fury to blurt out something that would be dangerous for the entire family. Fearful for themselves, they condemned her political activities and she became increasingly estranged from them.

A massive demonstration on 1 May 1905 in which Rambert took part and nearly got arrested, clinched the matter. She must be sent away. Her mother's sister lived in Paris, married to a Frenchman with the delightful name of Pierrot. It was hastily arranged that Rambert should go and stay with them, ostensibly for a holiday, but the parents had had enough of their tiresome fourth child and really wanted to be permanently rid of her. The Pierrots were both doctors and the plan was that Rambert should study medicine at the Sorbonne. Rambert did not take much persuading. Although she was not interested in medicine, it was impossible for a woman to go to university in Poland so she jumped at the opportunity. Besides, Paris! Irresistible. With hardly a backward glance Rambert set out on her journey, returning only for a brief visit in 1935 and again with her company after the Second World War.

CHAPTER 2

Rambert seems to have had no regrets or sentimentality about being parted from her family and yet it is probable that the absence of love and attention throughout her childhood must have hurt more than she would ever admit. But it was not in her nature to waste time going up the blind alleys of reproach or blame. The young woman who arrived in springtime Paris was hungry for life, possessed of an insatiable curiosity and unlimited reserves of enthusiasm and energy. She was breathing the air of a free country where people spoke the language they wanted to speak, where booksellers sold works from the whole world without restraint. Once she had left Poland she turned her back on the country of her birth, and her family from whom she became increasingly estranged when they realised that she had no intention of returning.

Suddenly life was fun. Relieved to have got away from the heavily-charged atmosphere of Polish politics, she revelled in a city dedicated to enjoyment and style, the city of the Comédie Française, of Sarah Bernhardt, Yvette Guilbert, Marcel Proust, Colette (whom she was later to meet), of the Impressionists, of Ravel, Debussy – the list was endless. And everyone dressed up, even the little girls playing croquet in the Bois de Boulogne. Their large-brimmed hats trimmed with ribbons and feathers must have reminded Rambert of the beloved hat of her childhood.

Rambert would never be mistaken for a Polish woman. Her bright eyes, like shiny black boot buttons, her black hair and even her lack of height gave no hint of her origins. From now on Myriam Rambam became first Marie Ramberg and finally, noting the French pronunciation of this name, Rambert.

Parisian life held everything she needed to nurture her mind and develop her taste. The impact of the city itself on an impressionable and still unsophisticated young woman was dramatic. She was moved by the grandeur of great houses, the elegance of columns, arches, wide tree-lined boulevards. In 1905 the motor car had not yet invaded the splendour of an age that harkened back to 'La Belle Époque'. Had it not been for the outbreak of the First World War it is certain that Rambert would have made France her home. It fitted her temperament far better than England ever could, where the insularity and ambiguous character of the English middle classes among whom she would live and work infuriated and frustrated her.

While Rambert in her memoir writes only what is absolutely necessary about her own parents she positively glows with warmth and affection for her uncle and aunt. They treated her like a daughter, it was the best thing that could possibly have happened to her. They were both hard-working doctors with a great many patients not all of whom could pay. They were on visiting terms with Pierre and Marie Curie who lived on the same street. Aunt Pierrot particularly, being Polish, was welcomed by Marie Curie who loved and missed her native land. Rambert's uncle, a mild man, was a follower of Kropotkin, a Russian prince who preached anarchism. This sounds alarming but apart from being thrown into prison for three days Uncle Pierrot was pretty harmless and confined himself to bringing free medical treatment to the poor and needy. Presumably their niece received an allowance from her parents, for the Pierrots were not well off. Nevertheless they took her to theatres and art galleries – the latter being a facet of her education that seems to have been neglected in Poland.

Mim was relieved to find that she was too young to study medicine and so she was enrolled for a one-year course for the Certificat d'Études Françaises at the Sorbonne. Foreign women were highly regarded at the Sorbonne which has been described as a 'microcosm of the universe'. Mim entered wholeheartedly into the life of the university and had no problem making friends. She perfected her French and threw herself into the social life of Paris. She was bombarded by exciting impressions and the opinions of her fellow students at the Sorbonne. She was also introduced to rich and influential Parisians who enjoyed her vivacity and wit and invited her to dance at their smart social gatherings.

While going through the youthful process of finding her own identity, her revolutionary tendencies found an outlet in the form of playing the aesthete. She rejected the superficial trappings of materialism and displayed the typical earnestness and intolerance of an intelligent young woman. She became passionate about 'Art', and was most impressed when she met a shaggy-haired young man at a party clad in a Greek tunic, gold bandeau and open-toed sandals, and discovered he was Raymond Duncan, Isadora's brother. At his urging she eschewed make-up and wore a tunic but soon abandoned the sandals. Rambert was always to have a complex about her feet – unusually large in proportion to her size and worse, had no natural instep – which was to cause her much anguish when she seriously began to train for ballet.

Although surrounded by smartly dressed people, she was firm in her espousal of the simple spartan life, besides, she didn't have much money, and tunics and sandals were cheaper than the elaborate toilettes of fashionable French women. Being young, she got away with it and for a short while created a stir and drew attention to herself by being 'different'. There was a vogue for free-style dance, in bare feet, with loosened hair held by a bandana, and loose-fitting draperies bound with gold filaments under the bosom and round the waist 'à la Duncan'. By her own admission Rambert danced about 'nothing in particular' and one can imagine that this kind of dancing without any foundation of technique might be considered self-indulgent and even embarrassing in these more sophisticated times. But dance was an important expression of freedom for the women of the early part of the century. Isadora was urging them to throw off their bras and corsets, appear unmade-up *à la naturelle* and generally indulge in physical freedom. The Greek tunics and heavy emotional content of free dance perfectly reflected this new attitude. Isadora herself was the only one who really got away with such a personal way of dancing that was impossible for others to reproduce.

I recall listening to a talk by Rambert to the Friends of Covent Garden some time in the sixties. Surprisingly she compared Duncan to the great classical dancer Anna Pavlova in that they both wanted to dance in their own way unfettered by any authority. They both had extraordinary talent, but the subject matter of their dances was so bad that only their genius made it acceptable. However, since Isadora danced in flimsy clinging material, bare-legged and bare-footed, and furthermore possessed a beautiful, voluptuous body it is not hard to conclude that part of her attraction was sexual. Rambert on the other hand was skinny with a small bosom and, although attractive, there was never a hint of sexuality or even sensuousness in her dancing, although she appreciated it in others.

In an age when dancing had sunk to the level of the artistic bordello, Isadora placed it on a par with religion, an act of worship. She was on a crusade to spread her own particular gospel without any deliberate attempt at entertaining her audience, merely wanting to convert them. She had a kind of evangelistic commitment that was typically American and she had an enormous influence on a whole new generation of dancers and choreographers.

Rambert became something of a vogue with artists, painters and 'le tout Paris' – fashionable, rich and famous people for whom she danced at soirées. She would always be a terrible snob, overawed at meeting influential people, particularly if they had titles, although she herself clung to her stance of aesthete and never over-indulged herself in luxury. She travelled quite a bit during those first years in Paris. She saw an ageing Loïe Fuller, the American dancer, who improvised, manipulating great swathes of silk, extending the length of her arms with sticks, and who could make herself into a flame, a flower, a witch or a goddess. Visiting a friend in Vienna, Rambert saw Ruth St Denis perform – more draperies, this time with an Indian slant, exotic make-up, great use of hands and arms, atmospheric music and lighting. The English Margaret Morris, another beautiful 'free' dancer, arrived in Paris in 1913 and she and her pupils were much in vogue among the artists.

On a visit to another friend, this time in Cannes, Mim took lessons from a teacher who taught acrobatics – this being probably where she perfected her cartwheels. She even rushed back to Poland for a hurried visit when she discovered Isadora was performing in Warsaw. It was on this occasion that she pushed her way through the stage door and threw herself unannounced into Isadora's dressing room and insisted on visiting her the next day to seek her advice. Isadora must have found this pushy young woman tiresome, she was not interested in her dancing and merely advised her to marry and raise a family, the last thing that Rambert wanted to hear.

One of her friends advised her to take ballet lessons in order to acquire some technique. Wafting around was all very well but it was a limiting form of dance and she was getting nowhere other than creating a little diversion after supper and meeting with some resistance from her hostesses when she asked to be paid a hundred francs for her performance.

She started to attend ballet lessons at the Paris Opéra under the tutelage of a teacher with the unfortunate name of Madame Rat, which must have provoked in private some entertainingly witty *bon mots* from Rambert, particularly as she did not like this teacher. Besides being rather scornful of Madame Rat's 'bourgeois' personality she heartily disliked the old-fashioned, sugary French style that had changed little since the days of Degas. After a short while, unimpressed as ever by classical ballet, she returned to her barefoot dancing.

All of this exciting formative period came to a full stop when Rambert became ill with acute appendicitis. The long and often painful convalescence temporarily put paid to her career as a dance recitalist. Weakened by the operation she felt listless and depressed and at a loss to know what to do with her life. She'd been dropped by her society friends, the novelty for them and for herself had played itself out. She had to live in a kind of Girls' Friendly Society hostel because her Aunt Pierrot, having also been ill, had gone away to recuperate. In any case it is possible that her niece had outstayed her welcome, perhaps it was expected that since she was now twenty it was high time for her to marry and 'settle down'.

Looking for a new opportunity she heard through one of the girls in the hostel of a Monsieur Dalcroze who was holding a summer course in Geneva in something called Eurythmics. Why not accompany her? It sounded interesting so Rambert decided to go too.

CHAPTER 3

Émile Jaques-Dalcroze was Swiss by nationality, born in Vienna, a music theoretician who through his experience of teaching singers founded a system of developing musical sensitivity to rhythm involving the body performing simple exercises. He improvised the musical accompaniment since, being unpredictable, it alerted a more spontaneous and concentrated physical response. He called his method Gymnastique Rythmique.

He heartily disliked ballet as did all the 'Moderns' (they still do). The distortions of the body, the stilted and mannered style of the ballet were anathema to the 'free' dancers and teachers. There were, however, some contradictions in his theories for while advocating 'free' dancing he nonetheless insisted on a rigid adherence to musical rhythm, the dancer or singer having proper regard to the composer's directions. Perhaps in his youth Monsieur Dalcroze had been subjected to those 'Soirées Musicales' so beloved of hostesses where full-bosomed ladies sang to captive audiences. Trembling with emotion, they warbled interminable renderings of Delilah yearning for her Samson, hanging on to favourite notes long after the composer intended. To Dalcroze's mind such liberties were inadmissible. He decided to impose on his pupils a rigid discipline to this effect.

As with all theories concerned with the arts, Dalcroze 's viewpoint was limited, but at this stage in Rambert's development the strict adherence to tempi demanded in 'Eurythmics' (as it later became known) was exactly what she needed. Instead of the two classes a day for which she had enrolled she took six!

Monsieur Jaques was a rather lovable little man; rotund, dapper, with twinkling eyes, tiny feet, splendid waxed moustaches and a neat imperial beard. By 1909 he was already middle-aged and his reputation was growing fast among musicians from all over the world. He had many characteristics similar to Mim which immediately endeared him to her – his infectious enthusiasm and dedication, and his wit, which often reduced her to fits of the giggles. His remarks were not always appreciated by his more intense acolytes, his gift of wit would surface in Rambert's teaching later on with her own pupils at the Mercury – also not always appreciated. Dalcroze was a brilliant mimic and possessed the actor's power of gesture which would have assured him success in live theatre had he so wished.

This was a carefree, happy time for Rambert. The environment itself contributed to her happiness. Who would not be happy to study in the shadow of great snow-capped mountains, to inhale the pure sparkling air of Lake Geneva? There were none of the tantrums and rebellious outbursts of the past nor the anguishing frustrations lying in wait in the future. And she had the company of like-minded young people who were there for musical education even if not necessarily gifted for dance.

Dalcroze related movement entirely to rhythm – a rather narrow approach. To him dancing was a kind of visual notation of music which was the dominant force. This was in conflict with dancers, who insist that the music should be subservient to the dance, a point of view that has often led to battles with pianists and conductors, not the least of these being between Rambert herself and her own conductors when later she had her own company. Choreographers' reactions to Dalcroze's method were varied. Michel Fokine hated it, calling it 'Rhythomania', on the other hand, Léonide Massine, arguably the greatest choreographer of the twentieth century, worked along the lines of Dalcroze when composing his symphonic ballets such as *Les Présages* to Tchaikovsky's Fifth Symphony and *Choreartium* to Brahms' Fourth. However, neither Antony Tudor nor Balanchine would consider it. Mary Wigman, who started the German expressionist dance movement, was to study with Dalcroze in later years but there would always be controversy over his theories.

The actual classes were very basic for the first year of training: walking, running, making specific and exact hand and even finger movements, running and stopping on given counts, turning or nodding the head, hopping, skipping, counting out the bars and above all sticking rigidly to the dictates of the rhythm extemporised by Monsieur Jaques at the piano. Whereas in the past Rambert had thrown herself into indulgent self-expression, reacting to whatever mood and emotions the music stirred within her, she now found the discipline a startling revelation, sometimes tying her in knots and reducing her to helpless laughter when she became totally confused. Dalcroze saw in this passionate, intelligent young woman a promising follower who brought her own perceptions to his limited knowledge of dance. Presumably relying on her parents to support her, she did not have much money and after a year she was granted a scholarship.

Although she had learnt to play the piano in Poland, by her own admission she was not very good. Now she had to improvise on the piano, read a score and, when Dalcroze accompanied the movers, they had to identify the key in which he was playing. There being no dancing as such

Mim at times became frustrated and would 'spill over' into something expressive and free. She found the restriction almost intolerable, whereupon her mentor would accuse her of being superficial, 'exteriorising' for effect. It was of course the intellectual approach which appealed to that side of Rambert's nature but it often came into conflict with her emotional side.

Dalcroze had many male pupils; musicians and conductors studying rhythm, some of them quite elderly. *La petite danseuse* with the sparkling eyes must have been regarded as something of an attraction and no doubt she had to lock her bedroom door at night even though she basked in their admiration. However, Mim's photographs and descriptions are entirely of women. It was the beginning of the 'new woman' age. They were all middle class, over eighteen, well educated and financially independent. Dalcroze's girls wore black bathing costumes for class, the respectable, unrevealing sort but quite daring for those days since they had bare arms and legs.

At the end of the first year Dalcroze requested from his pupils an essay on a subject of their own choosing. He was such a charismatic teacher that Mim had at first been enslaved by his theories on music and movement but now a small voice inside herself began to question. Worried at her own disloyalty she wrestled with the problem of the domination of rhythm and the phrasing of music. Then she came to a simple conclusion; Terpsichore, the Muse of dance, whom she considered was kept in the shadow by her sister Muses, would go it alone. Dance did not need music at all, it could stand on its own feet! She chose this theme for her essay and Dalcroze on reading it was furious and severely reprimanded her for her heresy.

It was the custom for the pupils to kiss their teacher on the cheek at the start and the end of the day. Rambert sulked and avoided him by going straight into the studio without greeting him. One day by chance she came face to face with him walking along the street. As he approached he pulled out a handkerchief and pretended to cry, dabbing his eyes and blowing his nose. The passers- by looked at him with such astonishment that Mim burst out laughing and rushed up to him giving him a kiss. After that there was no more talk of Terpsichore who was firmly locked away at the back of Rambert's mind to be released at a later date.

Although she didn't know it at the time Mim was instinctively following a trend expanded by Mary Wigman 'who subordinated music, almost discarding it in favour of percussive instruments and did not lean on music for emotional meaning'. Rambert never developed her ideas, unlike Wigman who became a great teacher in Germany and who influenced the entire contemporary dance movement. Mim simply did not have the temperament to stick doggedly to theories, she was always to be blown about by the winds of change and fashion. This was her weakness and her strength. Never bigoted, always open to new ideas and interested in new developments, she was the ideal channel through which her choreographers passed.

The banishment of her dance without music theory by her teacher did not alter Mim's private opinion and it was to surface again in the 60s when she gave a lecture to her own school. The students listened impassively to Mim, who with her wonderful grasp of words and gesture expanded on the fate of poor Terpsichore. Since they were studying classical ballet the young students, whose one ambition was to dance in a great company, were unsympathetic to the idea of dispensing with Tchaikovsky, Chopin and all the other wonderful composers to whose music they longed to dance. They applauded politely and retired to their dressing-rooms arguing indignantly. Afterwards Rambert cornered me and asked me what I thought of her theory. While I thought percussion and general sounds could be interesting the thought of a whole evening of dance without any sound at all alarmed me. I didn't have the courage to question her, in spite of now being a teacher I was still in awe of 'Madame'. Coward that I was, I ducked the question and retreated into the time-honoured escape line that her theory was interesting but that I would have to think about it. She must have been disappointed in me.

A realisation of her ideas was made by Christopher Bruce in 1972 when he choreographed ...*for these who die as cattle* whose title comes from the Wilfred Owen poem 'Anthem for Doomed Youth'. It was an interesting, dramatic work demanding enormous concentration from the audience, and it worked but the tension generated by silence only broken now and then with the noise of shuffling or stamping feet left me, and I think the audience, exhausted. A fascinating 'one-off' that to a certain extent vindicated Rambert's theory.

Only after the first year's indoctrination did Monsieur Jaques allow his students to extemporise movement to a theme devised by himself and accompanied by himself, a brilliant musician. Sometimes his witticisms had a sting in the tail. When a boringly lethargic Swiss girl came forward to do her piece he called out, 'Come now, Simone, give us a bloodbath called Caligula.'

When it came to the turn of a very shy and sexually inhibited German girl he wickedly shouted, 'No, no, Hans, I cannot, I am afraid!'

To Rambert he lowered his voice. 'Come now, my sombre one, my passionate one, give us Clytemnestra.'

It is interesting to see Mim through his eyes. He divined in her a quality that was never fulfilled. She would have made a splendid dramatic actress although it is difficult to picture that diminutive firebrand as a Clytemnestra.

Rambert now began to teach. The subject of her classes was something called *Turnen* – a German word for gymnastics. In spite of her teacher's dislike of ballet she managed to sneak in some of the classical barre-work and *port de bras* that she had learnt in Poland and from Madame Rat. There was a certain amount of ambiguity in her pose as *Danseuse Classique*. At that stage she didn't know very much of the classical technique and indeed claimed to dislike it herself, but it didn't stop her from wearing rather strange ballet slippers with ribbons crisscrossing half-way up her calves. Her pupils, however, remained bare-footed. Classical barre-work in bare feet is very painful and one imagines there must have been a certain amount of grumbling and rubbing of toes. This must have been a hotch-potch of a class but Mim was in a bit of a dance muddle herself at this point in her life.

Her gift for inventing dance 'out of nothing' was invaluable when demonstrations were mounted and she proved the perfect vessel, submitting to Dalcroze and his musical inventions. But it was as a pedagogue that he particularly interested her; she said that he was a builder of character. With her powerful gifts of observation she took a lot from him and would always acknowledge her debt to him.

Dalcroze was not particularly appreciated by the directors of the Conservatoire, who probably regarded him and his followers as harmless cranks, so they shed no tears when at the end of the first year the school moved to a splendid purpose-built establishment in Hellerau near Dresden. (The Conservatoire was later to regret its mistake in under-valuing him.) The numerous studios were large and airy, there were living quarters for the teachers, a huge central hall with a stage, and the setting in the grounds was idyllic. There were regular foreign visitors to the centre who watched classes and demonstrations.

In 1912, Rambert's last year, Prince Volkonsky, an enlightened former director of the Russian Imperial theatres, invited Dalcroze to bring a small group of his pupils including Mim to mount lecture-demonstrations in St Petersburg and Moscow. The performances were put on mainly for academies, institutes, and delightfully in St Petersburg for 'the young ladies of the nobility.' The interest in Dalcroze's work came from the drama side of Russian Theatre.

For these performances the pupils in the interests of decency abandoned the bathing costumes in favour of black jumpers, short black pleated skirts, long black stockings kept up with suspenders, and short black knickers. Rambert at twenty-two must have chafed at this unbecoming get-up and forgot to put the knickers on at the first demo in front of the Dowager Empress. She didn't realise this until she was already on the stage of the Mikhailovsky Theatre crawling about rhythmically on her stomach. The skirt gradually began to ride up revealing the suspenders to the delight of the gentlemen in the audience and to the horror of Rambert. In the nick of time she ignominiously crawled off the stage accompanied by furious hisses from Dalcroze at the piano.

The image of six earnest, nubile young women starting the demo in a circle lying on their fronts, gradually rising to a rhythmic beat then prancing around the stage showing their suspenders must have bemused Russians accustomed to the glamorous and heavily bejewelled costumes of the ballet. However, in Moscow, Stanislavsky, who was then working out his own experiments at the Arts Theatre showed great interest in Dalcroze's work.

Rambert showed no interest whatsoever in seeing the Imperial Ballet at the Maryinsky, perhaps almost like going to Rome and not visiting St Peter's. The age of Marius Petipa, who had died only two years previously, was still flourishing and great dancers such as Legat, Pavlova, Karsavina, Nijinsky and Fokine had danced on that magic stage. Had she asked it is certain that she could have been taken on a tour of the school, but no, her mind was focused on the drama. She nearly burst with joy in Moscow when she watched from a box performances of the Moscow Arts Theatre. She had the advantage over many of her colleagues that she understood and spoke Russian and the group met 'as friends' Stanislavsky himself and Olga Knipper and Gordon Craig, whose staging of *Hamlet* became world famous.

It seems odd that Mim ignored Russian ballet in favour of Russian drama when she was to be the founder of English ballet. And yet perhaps not so odd when one realises that it was that very interest in drama and free dance that fashioned the woman whose eclecticism encouraged the experiments of new young choreographers in the avant-garde of English dance. The group performed in Germany on the way back to Hellerau and routine. The trip to Russia had stirred Rambert and she settled back with difficulty. She knew it was time for her to move on, but to what? It seems that this had already been decided for her.

There was the usual influx of visitors that year and she did not pay any attention to two people who sat in on several of her classes one day. One of them was a tall, dark, heavy man and the other a much smaller man with indeterminate features. The students were accustomed to being watched; they were simply pawns to Dalcroze's techniques. It was therefore a great surprise to Mim to be called to Dalcroze's office and introduced to Serge Diaghilev and Vaslav Nijinsky. She was even more surprised when Diaghilev suggested that she might be of service to Nijinsky who was embarking on a new work to rhythmically complicated music.

Wildly excited she immediately agreed to Diaghilev's invitation to come to Berlin where the company was performing. Diaghilev she noticed did all the talking – Nijinsky simply nodded his head and kissed her hand in true Polish fashion on their departure.

Chapter 4

The love affair with Eurythmics could not last. Diaghilev rescued Rambert just in time for she would never have been content to remain a Eurythmics teacher. This episode turned out to have been simply part of her journey towards ballet and it took the Diaghilev company to achieve this. Her three years with Dalcroze although certainly not wasted had delayed her involvement with ballet. At twenty-three she was too old even to consider becoming a professional classical dancer and she would always regret that she could never make up for those precious lost years of early training.

Diaghilev with his unique perspicacity had noted that apart from being Dalcroze's star pupil her grasp of Russian – and indeed French and Polish, would be an asset in teaching his predominantly Russian company. At Diaghilev's invitation she travelled to Berlin to watch a performance. The programme consisted of two Fokine ballets, *Carnaval* which she adored, *Cléopâtre* which she had the temerity to criticise, and Nijinsky's *L'Après-midi d'un faune* which she thought unmusical. She was never slow to voice her opinion, asked for or not, and candour invariably overruled tact. She had the typical chutzpah of her Jewish ancestry and it was certainly very cheeky to complain that the dancers in the procession in *Cléopâtre* did not march in time to the music – Fokine did not intend that they should. It was a good job for her that the great and choleric Fokine himself was not there as he would certainly have put this pushy little young woman in her place.

She couldn't understand Nijinsky's treatment of Debussy's wonderful music. 'He completely ignores it!' she expostulated to Diaghilev. He did not defend Fokine since they had fallen out at that time but her criticism of Nijinsky must have smarted. Of course she was being loyal to her indoctrination by Dalcroze and later she would understand both choreographers and blush at the memory of her ignorant observations.

Over a working supper it was decided that she would join the company in Budapest in order to help Nijinsky and the company with the complicated rhythms of his new ballet *Le Sacre du printemps* to a new score by Igor Stravinsky. Diaghilev engaged Rambert as adviser in the Dalcroze method and she was fortunate in that the specialised nature of the work gave her a status that she would not have had as a humble apprentice dancer working at the back of the corps de ballet. Diaghilev did not take her seriously as a dancer, although it was understood that she would make herself useful in some of the ballets.

The Russians, unlike the British, did not demand exact uniformity of height or type for their dancers. For instance, short girls and boys were used by Fokine as character dancers for the wild, fast sequences of such ballets as *Prince Igor*, *Schéhérazade* and *The Firebird*. Therefore in spite of the lack of a classical training it was quite plausible for Rambert to be in those ballets and of course she would have to join in crowd scenes for such ballets as *Petrushka*.

She spent her first days in Budapest watching performances and, most importantly, rehearsals. It is not hard to imagine the reactions of this bright-eyed, observant little person sitting on the sidelines watching a large company of superb dancers rehearsing marvellously conceived ballets, some of them classics in perpetuity. It was quite awe-inspiring and not a little intimidating to someone without experience of such professionalism, who presumably had never watched a full-scale rehearsal. She was at once elated, excited and amused by the combustible Russians, bored with rehearsing long-established ballets, jostling each other, arguing over the execution of certain passages. The raised voices of squabbling women, the heat, the sweat pouring out of threshing, leaping bodies, the sudden halt and silence while a sequence was remembered and worked out was more reminiscent of a building site, and in a way the reconstruction of a ballet is just that. In the days before dance notation and with the absence of the choreographer it was left to the older dancers to recall the steps, the patterns and the musical phrasing, not always accurately.

Mim watched avidly, her sharp black eyes taking in every move, every instruction, mouth pursed, frowning – a characteristic expression that would intimidate many dancers in the future who did not understand that this was simply concentration. Above the din she noted, not always approvingly, the long-suffering rehearsal pianist hammering out the music of Rimsky-Korsakov, Stravinsky, Tchaikovsky, on an old upright piano, chain-smoking pungent smelling Russian cigarettes.

Dominating the scene was the voice of Serge Grigoriev, '*Icheras, sama snatchala*' (Once again from the beginning) repeated again and again. Grigoriev, then twenty-six years old, had joined the company for the first season in Paris in 1909 and as Régisseur was to remain right up to Diaghilev's death. Trained initially at the Maryinsky Theatre in St Petersburg, he knew the entire repertoire and enjoyed Diaghilev's absolute trust. Diaghilev said of him, 'Grigoriev is the only member of my ballet company who is indispensable.' A lovable giant of a man, he had the round eyes of a child, a long nose that ended with a tilt as though it had changed its mind, a humorous mouth and an endearing slight lisp, created perhaps by the uneven distribution of his teeth.

The volatile, temperamental Russian dancers were not easy to control, but he understood them. Always sympathetic to their needs, he listened to their troubles like a father, coaxing a rebellious young man back into the studio, calming the tantrums of the ballerina, comforting a tearful older woman of the corps de ballet. They were his children and they adored him. Sometimes he would lose his patience and with a great roar of exasperation, only equalled by Fokine, he would bring the entire rehearsal to a standstill. After a sharp lecture the dancers would meekly return to their places and start all over again.

It was initially arranged that Rambert would give classes in the Dalcroze technique for the company, but it was plain from the first session that this was not a good idea. Tired from Cecchetti's demanding classes and the rehearsals, they were in no mood to co-operate and to expect the greatest dancers in the world, exquisitely trained at the Imperial Russian school, to go back to the nursery was more than they could tolerate. Here was this young woman treating them like students, asking them to walk about counting the rhythm like an elementary lesson in arithmetic. Not being a classical dancer herself, she would not have understood how tiring that kind of laborious walking, hopping and skipping is to a body trained for speed. Furthermore they loathed both Stravinsky's score and Nijinsky's unconventional choreography. Rambert was shrewd and intuitive enough to understand their reactions and it was decided to scrap the classes.

How much did the Dalcroze theories help the dancers to decipher the Stravinsky music for *Sacre*? They had already experienced his rhythmically complicated music for *Petrushka* and *The Firebird* so they were sophisticated and adaptable, even though they may have disliked the music. It was Nijinsky himself who benefited most from Rambert's assistance. Stravinsky was insistent that there should be a step on every beat – which was in complete contrast to Debussy's *L'Après-midi* where the nymphs walked steadily across the stage using the great surges of melody as background.

It was surely the movement rather than the music that upset the dancers. In the late twentieth century Martha Graham aroused much controversy and indeed ridicule with her use of the upturned foot and the parallel position of the feet. Nijinsky in *L'Après-midi* was way ahead of his time and encountered opposition from his dancers, and in *Sacre* his demands were an affront to the classical tradition in which they had been nurtured.

When even present-day classical purists dislike contemporary dance, how much more shocking it must have seemed to both the dancers and the Parisian *beau monde* who attended that first night in 1912. They reacted violently to Nijinsky's choreography which was based on his concept of the primitive East European peasant. The exaggerated turn-out, the harmonious line of the arms, the lightness, the perfect alignment of the leg in the arabesque terminating in the tapered foot were jettisoned in favour of a knock-kneed, turned-in position of the legs, awkward jerky spasms, angularity, spatula-shaped hands, the introverted stance of the uncouth serf-peasant. This was not like character dancing where the body moved with naturalness to melodic, identifiable rhythms, but here the dancers were ordered to move heavily, close up the body, twist and distort, and count every remorseless note.

The exasperated dancers were made even more miserable by numerous conflicts between composer and choreographer. Nijinsky was a slow worker, incapable of explaining in words what he wanted, so the dancers had to copy him exactly. He demanded blind obedience and if they showed the slightest inclination to express themselves individually he would fly into a rage. There were in all 120 rehearsals, a luxury no present day company could afford. Rambert was kept busy acting as répétiteur, taking individuals away to coach them at the end of the rehearsal, and above all helping Nijinsky with praise and encouragement. Rambert the rebel recognised the rebel in Nijinsky. His was a totally personal interpretation of dance – Fokine had started the rebellion, Nijinsky carried it farther – too far for his time.

The company eventually overcame their difficulties and the dancing was magnificent, but it did not save the ballet. John Fletcher, an enthusiastic American who saw the performance in Paris, wrote to Cyril Beaumont the critic that, 'Nijinsky was greater than Fokine and that *Sacre* was the most savage, original, gorgeous thing the Diaghilev ballet had ever done.' He added that London would probably laugh at it, but more politely since the English ballet public had always been better behaved than the French.

Rambert writes with enchantment of that historic and disastrous first night in Paris. After the performance she accompanied her friends on a joyous and hilarious night out, almost as though they were all delighted *Sacre* had been a failure. She herself was on a high, entirely concerned with herself, and she expressed no sympathy for Nijinsky. Normally someone who has been involved with a production as intimately as she was, would feel a sense of disappointment, even weep, that a child should be stillborn, but there appears to have been none of this.

Sacre and Nijinsky himself had a profound influence on Rambert's life, she never forgot her time with Diaghilev and talked at length about it for the rest of her life. She recognised Nijinsky's genius as choreographer before most other people of that period. The fact that *Sacre* was dropped from the repertoire after only six performances (three in London) suggests that even Diaghilev's faith was faltering.

After Paris the company went to London for a season at Drury Lane Theatre. Rambert was not particularly impressed with London. In her eyes it compared poorly with her adored Paris which in 1912 she considered her home. So much of a touring company's time is taken up with rehearsing and performing that the most that is seen of a city is the area between the lodgings and the theatre and sheer exhaustion precludes sightseeing. There were probably some parties to which the company were invited but otherwise she met few people and she would have been surprised, even indignant, had she been told that soon London would be her home. Why on earth should she want to live in a city that as far as she could tell was regularly hidden under a blanket of thick, foul fog?

Rambert was still with the company when they embarked on the South American tour in August 1913. Several of the members decided not to go and these places had to be filled. It was a tradition with the Russian ballet to occasionally take in the dancing daughters of rich patrons who were allowed to participate in the ensembles and take Maestro Cecchetti's classes, travelling at their own expense and receiving no salary. One such was a beautiful Hungarian girl, Romola de Pulsky, who at the last minute applied to be included in the tour.

The sea voyage took 22 days, during which time the dancers relaxed and lazed about in the sun. Rambert travelled third class and there is a delightful photograph taken on deck of tiny Mim sandwiched between three tall women dressed in long white cambric dresses and holding each other round the waist. Rambert frequently visited her friends, the conductor René Baton and his wife, who were travelling first class, and this gave her the opportunity to meet Nijinsky. Diaghilev was not on board and neither was his tiresome valet Vasili who had constantly interrupted private rehearsals of *Sacre* on some pretext or other, obeying Diaghilev's orders never to leave Nijinsky alone with Rambert. Now at last they felt free to enjoy each other's company.

She said later in life that she had been in love with Nijinsky and certainly this strange, inarticulate man who bit his fingernails was able to confide in Rambert. She had a perceptiveness and intuitive capacity to draw out a person's innermost and repressed thoughts. They spoke together in Polish and had much in common, being almost the same age. They had both been brought up in Czarist Warsaw, which he had left at the age of ten to join the Maryinsky ballet school. Rambert worshipped his talent and he in his turn found someone who understood his turbulent, restless nature and his moods. He was a lost creature held in an unwelcome alliance with the domineering, powerful and possessive Diaghilev who harnessed Nijinsky's talent to his own and to his company's glory.

What did they talk about on those gentle promenades round the deck, lying about in deckchairs in the sultry heat? Art, literature, life and – love? Did Mim perhaps gently suggest to him that a liaison with a woman was preferable to a liaison with a man? Perhaps she influenced him more than she realised, only to discover painfully that his thoughts on this subject were on another – the beautiful rich girl who occupied the stateroom opposite his, Romola de Pulsky.

Mim had met Romola in Paris and thought it quite natural that she should share her own adoration of Nijinsky. It was a piquant situation, neither of them realising the other was in love with him. Mim would join Romola in her state room and chatter about Nijinsky, proudly and happily divulging information about their idol's tastes, points of view and aspirations, the while brushing Romola's long blonde hair. Romola of course was making use of Mim who could communicate with him. Romola only spoke French and Nijinsky's French was almost non-existent. 'How can you talk to him?' Rambert asked, 'We manage', Romola answered with a secret smile.

Rambert was flattered to be a friend of Romola, an amiable dilettante dabbling in art, a person of breeding. She was always attracted to wealth and good birth – and most importantly, not being a great beauty herself she was unrestrained in her admiration of beauty. Romola's actress mother had no doubt taught her the artifices of the theatre and she had the special look of a woman who had money to spend on herself, an image that stirred the romanticism in Nijinsky. For him Rambert was a colleague, but Romola of the long blonde hair was the Sleeping Beauty personified, and this Beauty had decided to capture her Prince. It would seem that she had joined the South American tour for precisely that end.

On one of the last days of the voyage Nijinsky told Mim he was in love with Romola. Mim treated it as a joke – after all, he was Diaghilev's lover. But it was no joke. They became engaged and subsequently in Rio de Janeiro they married. Rambert found herself thrust aside by his entourage and he hardly gave her a backward glance. She relates how desperately unhappy she was and even contemplated throwing herself overboard. This melodramatic act would not have fitted Rambert's character, but she was capable of momentary passion during which she suffered acutely.

Nijinsky's subsequent dismissal after marrying may very well have suited Diaghilev. Karsavina wrote; 'hardly had his cultivation of a new talent flowered than he shifted his interest to a new discovery'. So it happened with Nijinsky. But what of Marie Rambert? Her impact on the Diaghilev company was of no importance. What was important was the impact of the Diaghilev company on Marie Rambert and she remained loyal to the memory of Nijinsky all her life.

Chapter 5

Rambert's contract was not renewed after the South American tour for she was no longer useful to the company. A year is not long with a ballet company, but for her it was sufficient. No school or academy could have taught her the Diaghilev concept of ballet which shone like an illuminated flight path for her to follow on her own journey in presenting ballet as an art form. She understood that good dancing was not enough, that as well as gifted choreographers the ballet needed great composers and designers, and the audience must be transported into a fantasy world only made possible by the magic of total theatre.

She also perceived that choreographers needed guidance and, noting Diaghilev's ruthlessness in giving that guidance, she realised there must be no compromises. Talent had to be cultivated by instilling taste, opening horizons, refining the mind, firing imagination. Also, having listened to the protests and criticisms of Diaghilev by his volatile company, she understood the enforced isolation of directorship. Popularity was of secondary importance in the quest for quality and perfection. But she could not imitate Diaghilev, she had to find her own way.

There is no knowing how deeply Rambert was hurt by the *affaire* Nijinsky. She was such an unusual mixture. Although on occasions embarrassingly vociferous in her public life she kept her own counsel in anything appertaining to her personal life. Generally possessed of a resilient nature she was nevertheless plagued by devastating attacks of migraine, lasting sometimes as long as three days when she would stay in bed in a darkened room. This seems to have been the only weakness in an otherwise healthy constitution.

She was now finally set on her own course and once back in Paris she lost no time. It was imperative that she continue taking classes in the classical technique and, in spite of her reservations, she returned to the Opéra and Madame Rat. Having taken the daily Maestro Cecchetti classes in the company, she had now become sufficiently discriminating to pull out the sound points of Madame's teaching and ignore the rest. She had learnt, from watching Nijinsky and Karsavina in class, the importance of total commitment and gruelling, slogging hard work. There was to be no more prancing around in Greek draperies, from now on she was deadly serious.

But for the time being she had to support herself, so she returned to making solo appearances with a new programme of dances. Armed with a letter of introduction from Colette Willy whom she knew slightly she presented herself to the manager of the Théâtre Impérial in the Champs Élysées and he gave her two recitals. Thanks to the success of these she returned to appearing at soirées in private houses for which she was well paid. She made many useful contacts and also friends, including one who became her life-long friend, Vera Donnet.

There are certain people in a life who stand out as major influences and point the way ahead. Such a one was Vera Donnet. She was the daughter of wealthy landowners in the Ukraine, that marvellously rich agricultural land of black soil which grew the best wheat in Europe. Having been largely brought up by foreign governesses, she had fled her native land during the Russian revolution and settled in Paris until once again she fled, this time to England. She was possibly of Jewish descent; no one seems to have discovered her family name, although her patronymic was Arkadieva. Her first husband was Swiss and when later she moved to England she married Harold Bowen.

She had studied at Geneva University but Rambert first met her in Paris, probably at one of the soirées at which Rambert danced. Donnet was an attractive, cultured person of great charm and although she had no real talent she nevertheless considered herself a singer who no doubt entertained the guests at amateur soirées. She spotted an unusual person in Rambert, they had much in common, both émigrées, both spoke Russian and French, of the same age and both passionately interested in the arts. Chic, lively and intelligent, Vera was the perfect role model for Rambert, who later was to write, 'Her advice in art as well as in life was law to me – and I never ignored it.'

Mim had returned to Paris determined to grab life by the throat and, previously unconcerned by the cultivation of herself as a woman, she now with the help of Vera proceeded to put behind her the intellectual Isadora 'back-to-nature' image. Vera urged her to dress better, sent her to her couturière, advised her on the art of street make-up, and her thick black hair was pulled back from her brow into a chignon. Vera, who understood the value of presentation, pointed out to Rambert that her fee would increase with the improvement of her wardrobe. Rambert took to cramming her feet into heeled shoes and wearing turbans and feathered high hats to add the missing inches to her height. They met every day, went shopping together, perched on little gilded chairs in tea-rooms in the Champs Élysées drinking hot chocolate and exchanging gossip.

Vera also tried to teach her protégée good manners, without much success. Rambert tried to control her wayward tongue only to burst out with some devastating remark that she simply could not suppress particularly if someone in her opinion had said something stupid. Although her wit and charm were irresistible and people forgave her indiscretions she would always be careless of other people's feelings. Was she insensitive? Or was it simply that she could not disguise her own feelings and saw no reason to do so?

Rambert's new recital repertoire was now influenced by her experience with Diaghilev. Gone was the prancing around barefooted to Grieg. Now there were structured dances in the various styles she had learnt in *Sacre*, *Schéhérazade*, *Igor*, a Russian character dance in the style of the nursemaids in *Petrushka* and a passionate Chopin revolutionary study dressed all in white waving a banner bearing the Polish flag. Her costumes were well made and decorative and what may have been lacking in technique was compensated for by a lovely use of head and arms and a natural stage personality. She was a success and was invited to dinners and parties where she entertained her fellow guests with witty stories and hilarious *bon mots*. No doubt the tag 'former Diaghilev company' made her a sought-after and interesting guest. She never lost touch with her adored uncle and aunt and their children. There appears to have been no contact with her family in Warsaw.

In the summer of 1914 she took a holiday in Geneva, staying with friends and visiting her old teacher Dalcroze who greeted her with affection. She went to a round of parties but the imminence of war overhung what should have been a happy, carefree visit. As the news became bleaker she curtailed her visit, rushing back to be with the Pierrots. She was extremely distressed by the tense atmosphere in Paris and fearful for her aunt and uncle, particularly as the latter was due to be enlisted as soon as war broke out. On arrival at the Gare de l'Est she had a lot of trouble getting through the crowds milling around aimlessly, almost panic-stricken. Having no French francs she had to battle her way on foot, lugging her suitcase along the pavements and through the traffic.

By an extraordinary coincidence she found herself opposite a stationary taxi caught in the jam in which sat Vera Donnet in a smart hat adorned with an aigrette, almost hidden amongst a mountain of hat-boxes, starched blouses hastily rescued from the laundry and piles of luggage. Suddenly spotting Mim on the pavement she shouted to her to drop everything and come immediately to London, then disappeared with the ongoing traffic in the direction of the station.

Rambert stayed on in France until the German advance on Paris. She continued taking her daily ballet lesson and refused to acknowledge that the war could interfere with her life, but there were no more recitals and soon the government was advising people to leave the city. What went on in Rambert's mind? Did she have any thoughts of returning to her native land? It seems not. Vera was writing endless letters urging her to come to London, her uncle had already gone to serve at the Front, her cousins had been sent away to Brittany, her aunt insisted on staying behind to care for the sick and wounded in her role as doctor. All their friends had departed. It was only then, when everyone had gone away that Rambert faced up to her situation and made up her mind. She had to escape to England, and quickly. She packed what she could and made her way to Calais where she had to fight through the crowds to get on to the ferry – that dear old ferry so taken for granted by today's complacent English, but still the gateway to freedom across that narrow channel of water.

When it came to pushing Rambert had no equal. She could move with the speed of lightning and being small dart under people's arms without them even noticing. And she was ruthless when it came to getting what she wanted and what she wanted at that moment in her life was to be as far away from the Germans as possible. It's doubtful whether she foresaw any future for herself other than safety. That much her upbringing in Poland had taught her.

Chapter 6

The English ballet scene of 1914 was volatile and by one of those flukes of history Rambert arrived at just the right time. Attitudes towards ballet had been revolutionised by the advent of first Anna Pavlova and then the Diaghilev Ballet. Although the war temporarily interrupted further development there was a residue of interest that fired the imagination of influential people concerned with the arts and those dancers who found themselves stranded in England.

There had been very little happening in ballet during the beginning of the twentieth century, or indeed before. The Victorian influence still prevailed and the evolution of dance was hampered by social mores. The land of Shakespeare was not inclined to dance. While the bitter winters of Eastern Europe prompted its people to keep warm with copious draughts of vodka and energetic dancing, the British were crippled with rheumatism from the damp, and even in their youth were tight-hipped and tight-lipped. Both dancing and acting were considered slightly indecent and even sinful by the majority of the population. No 'nice' girls danced, it smacked of the harem, sex was sinful, and dancing exhibitionism of a doubtful kind. Ballerinas were mostly foreign since it was considered a foreign art not suitable for the English.

Adeline Genée, the Danish ballerina, had come to London in the late 1800s and occupied a special place in the hearts of the audiences of the Empire Theatre in Leicester Square, The standard of the corps de ballet was poor but provided a suitable background for the better-trained foreign visitors. The English dancers could not be persuaded to work hard, which is not surprising since they were never allowed to rise above corps de ballet level, pointe work had only been introduced in 1906 and was still in its tentative stage, the shoes were nothing like as hard as today's. Taglioni's pointe shoes were barely reinforced since she had such strong feet, the same could not be said of our early English dancers.

Since all the major dancers were imported there was no incentive, a talented girl could not expect to go farther than the front row. The members of the huge corps de ballet at the Empire came from the lower classes and were equipped with a scarcely adequate training. Their hopes were to catch the eye of wealthy men in the audience. In the previous century male roles had been danced by women, but although there were now more men dancing it was considered a rather peculiar occupation for a man. The back rows were occupied by amateurs, hangers-on, relations of stage carpenters, daughters of door-keepers and firemen. However, discipline was strict and negligence or unpunctuality were fined. The Empire corps de ballet had to look pretty and were required to stay in their dressing-rooms when not performing, a precaution perhaps against marauding men-about-town.

Although quite well paid, the work was not strenuous by modern standards. The repertoire of steps was limited and nothing much was expected of the dancers, most of whom were women, what men there were operated as 'porteurs', simply lugging the ballerina across the stage, invisible beneath the froth of the ballerina's tutu, which in those days was a respectable calf-length.

With the exception of the traditional ballets such as *Coppélia*, *Giselle* and *Sylvia* the ballets at the Empire were 'topical' depicting everyday themes. *Round the Town*, for instance, had a London setting depicting a school master showing his pupils the sights of London. When Cecchetti was imported, a critic wrote, 'I am afraid he is rather lost in Leicester Square where the audience who are capable of appreciating nothing more than acrobatics stare blindly at his finest entrechats.' Lydia Kyasht followed Genée, then Phyllis Bedells. In 1910 Russian guest artists started appearing at the Coliseum, the London Hippodrome and the Palace Theatre. This was followed by Anna Pavlova and her partner Mikhail Mordkin, Tamara Karsavina, Olga Preobrajenska, all of whom offered strong competition to the Empire.

The audiences considered that it was all right for Russians to dance, coming as they did from a strange far-off country, they were in any case half wild and only appealed to the limited audience of the intelligentsia. A turn on a music-hall stage well backed up by a large corps de ballet, pretty light music, elaborate costumes and scenery all jumbled up together was fine, but a whole evening of ballet was out of the question. The exception was Anna Pavlova. She brought a new concept of ballet to the masses, touring tirelessly up and down the country, first on her own appearing in provincial music-halls, and later with a small company of competent English dancers.

The Dying Swan was seen by countless mothers of small daughters who were inspired by this exquisite creature moving ghost-like in a blue light to expire at the end to the plaintive music of Saint-Saëns. Proud mothers beamed at the sight of their tiny tots hanging on to the dining-room table laboriously teetering round in bare feet 'on their toes'. They hurried along to their local dancing school and, regardless of the competence of the teacher, demanded that their little girl be put on pointe. Dressed in a little white ballet dress the child tottered around waving her arms up and down and sinking none too elegantly to the floor at the end. It was the women's enchantment with Pavlova that inspired them to send their daughters to be trained in ballet.

I recall a conversation in the sixties when Rambert complained that she had never had rich and influential friends, making the comparison with some other more fortunate contemporary. Nothing could have been further from the truth. She always had influential friends and indeed cultivated them. She was a consummate snob and fashionable society mattered a great deal to her as the proliferation of name-dropping in her memoir demonstrates.

She arrived in London with very little money but immediately got in touch with an English couple she had met at the Dalcroze Institute in Geneva. Mr and Mrs Ingham were a kindly couple and took Mim under their wing. He was now a director of the School of Eurythmics in London and found her work as a teacher both at the school and privately, going to people's houses to teach children. She also gave lessons in the French language and for a time took a job looking after children. One can imagine that this last would not have been much to her taste, she was hardly the nursemaid or even the mother type, although in her old age she enjoyed her own grandchildren.

Through teaching Eurythmics to the children of diplomats she got to know the parents and was often invited to their houses socially. She presumably had managed to bring her 'new look' wardrobe with her in her precipitate exit from Paris. The chic of these Parisian clothes coupled with her wit and charm made her a welcome guest at dinner tables. In spite of not being a conventionally beautiful woman her photographs reveal style in the way she holds herself, a consciousness of the position of the head and her expressive face leaps out of the picture. Her talent for using superlatives was inexhaustible and her enthusiasms were often exaggerated by much wringing of the hands and knitting of the brows. Although she claimed she never had any ambition to be an actress she certainly knew how to pull the stops out when she was 'on show'. Rambert was expected to sing for her supper and she did not fail her hosts, who thought her a fascinating acquisition. Her fractured English was amusing although she preferred to speak French, and this posed no problem in the upper-class households where she was entertained. A 'Mademoiselle' to teach children

French was essential at that period when this was the language of the salon and diplomacy. Rambert herself acted as a 'Mademoiselle' on one or two occasions when she was struggling to survive.

But beneath the showmanship was an anxious and somewhat lost young woman seeking to find a place for herself in a new environment. She had to earn her living somehow and for the next three years it must have been far from easy. She was twenty-six, unmarried, without a country and really, in spite of her education and intelligence, without a metier. Uprooted for the second time, having to adapt once again to a different society,she had no idea how to direct her life and was not quite independent enough to stand on her own feet, and she was hopeless about money. Modest in material demands, she had never wanted for anything, and immersed as she had been in her artistic loves and aspirations she had never really thought about the practical aspects of living. Fortunately, beneath that lively image lay a down-to-earth Polish woman who knew about hardship and in fact was quite spartan in her own day-to-day living. Although she relished the well-laden dinner tables of the rich she never drank spirits and hardly any wine, half a glass of which she claimed made her drunk, she was sparing with food to the point of parsimony and eschewed luxury to the point of discomfort.

She now set about establishing herself and finding somewhere to live. She was introduced to Mrs James Muirhead who invited her to lodge in her house for the duration of the war. And she looked around for a teacher. Seraphina Astafieva, a former dancer with Diaghilev, had opened her own studio in London and Rambert attended classes when she could. She was also introduced to Mabel Dolmetsch, an expert on authentic antique dances and Rambert studied with her for a while.

It was Vera Donnet who put Mim back on track. She was connected with the Stage Society, a group dedicated to producing plays of artistic merit but unlikely to be presented by a commercial management. They were usually staged in West End theatres but since the actors were professionals working during the week, the performances were on Sunday nights when actors and theatres were free. Donnet invited Rambert to collaborate with her in producing a ballet for which she had written the libretto. The ballet was to be called *La Pomme d'or* and the theme was to be the 'awakening of the medieval world to the Renaissance of humanism' – no small project. Although Donnet had produced some theatrical productions this was her first venture into what she termed ballet which, since there was no real dancing, we would call 'movement.' Although Rambert would never claim to be a choreographer, intellectually she understood the concept of the piece, based on the style of the Renaissance, gleaned from paintings and descriptions of the period. It was well researched and Mabel Dolmetsch proved a valuable source of information when it came to staging the dances of the period.

Rambert and Donnet succeeded between them in producing a work of rare quality which was staged at the Garrick Theatre in 1917 and achieved a remarkable success. There were eloquent write-ups in the London press and Rambert herself received ecstatic notices describing her as 'a fresh breath of spring'. This success brought Rambert to the public attention and in fact pointed the way to her future development. She had tasted the satisfaction of involvement in production and saw that although she would never make a career as a dancer, she would find compensation in guiding and directing other dancers. But for this it was essential she continue training and learn as much as possible about her craft.

Vera was concerned with Mim's future and was always ready with wise counsel. Vera, who herself was to remarry to an Englishman, emphasised to Rambert the importance of finding an English husband if she wanted to settle in England. There has always been, and still is, a myth about the English 'gent' in the eyes of Europeans. His immaculately cut Savile Row suit, his height, his drawl, his coolness and his elegance have always been admired and imitated the world over. He is a species much sought after by enterprising foreign ladies who do not take into account his phlegmatic nature which can drive his more fiery partner into frenzies of irritation – but more of that later.

Rambert co-produced two more productions with Donnet. *Fêtes Galantes* was a parody of manners of the eighteenth century in which Rambert played an exquisite French Marquise to perfection. She attracted rave notices in the press. In 1918 she again participated in an abstract ballet with the rather off-putting title *Ballet Philosophique*. The synopsis in the programme: 'Thought was, then the man, then love. Evil destroyed man and love. Thought alone survived' was no help. The ballet was pretentious and obscure. The pitfalls of such subjects for dance are legion and still meet with bemused and bored audiences lost in a wilderness of incomprehension. Donnet was undoubtedly a brilliant woman but in this case she overreached herself.

This was a valuable gestation period for Rambert and, helped immeasurably by Donnet, she had the opportunity to explore her own talents and capacities, something that also could not have happened without the help and support of the rich amateurs with whom she lived and worked. Later in life Rambert was to be scathing about 'amateurs' (which, incidently, in France means enthusiasts) but they were the very people who opened doors for her in those first years in London.

CHAPTER 7

In the autumn of 1917 Rambert was introduced to Ashley Dukes. She had been dimly aware of his name when *Pomme d 'or* was presented at the Ambassadors in February of that year, having noticed that he had done the translation of *The Man who married a Dumb Wife*. But since he was serving in Germany at the time she did not actually meet him until she found he rself sitting next to him at a dinner party.

During the first year of the war Mim had played her part in brightening up the lives of young officers on leave from the front: dining, being taken to the theatre, flirting harmlessly, probably allowing a chaste kiss, an arm around the waist, no more. These former public schoolboys, handsome in their smart uniforms, all of them brave young men, nonetheless bored her. She had nothing in common with them but she found Dukes more interesting. The son of a West Country clergyman, he had studied chemistry and physics at Manchester University. But while taking his finals and finishing as an honours graduate he had realised that these subjects did not hold any real interest for him, so he went to Munich to complete his education as a postgraduate in German philosophy. Both he and his two brothers served in the army for the whole of the war, Ashley rising to the rank of company commander.

He was thirty-two when Rambert met him, a tall, quite imposing man, somewhat pompous and overbearing. He nevertheless impressed her with his knowledge of theatre and literature. Furthermore, he had seen the Diaghilev Ballet in 1911 and no doubt Mim's previous involvement with the company fascinated him. She was very feminine and possessed enormous charm; coupled with which she was well educated, a brilliant conversationalist, and after his rather heavy assignment in war-ravaged Germany she brought into his life a breath of enchantment he could not resist. While abroad he had seen and fallen in love with her photograph as the Marquise in *Fêtes Galantes*. Rambert in her own memoir is disparaging of herself, commenting that it must have been most disillusioning to meet her without the clever make-up that Vera Donnet had devised for her. But Ashley couldn't have been too disappointed for he asked her to marry him.

The courtship was conducted mostly by letters and snatched moments together when he was on leave. They were married in 1918 but he was to spend another year abroad serving as a German-speaking officer. They married without consulting their respective parents – in fact their opinion was not sought. Rambert in any case was out of touch with her own family and Ashley's father had remarried after the tragic death of his wife when Ashley was a child and they lived away from London.

The wedding photograph shows Mim (who in her bare feet would hardly have come up to Ashley's shoulder) wearing satin lace-up high-heeled shoes, a voluminous satin coat and a most alarming tall coal-scuttle hat pulled down to her eyebrows, which certainly added to her height but not much else. Ashley, hands in pockets, looks pensively down at the hat perhaps wondering what he has taken on. Mim exulted in becoming a British citizen and even shouted 'God Save The King' to the astonishment of the registrar. True to form she refused to go off on honeymoon because her going-away costume was not ready. It was perhaps Ashley's first taste of the famous tantrums that he would have to endure during the whole of their married life. Marrying Ashley was the most important event in Rambert's life. Without his encouragement and support it is doubtful whether she would have found the courage to launch herself as a distinguished pioneer of the Renaissance of English ballet.

Once demobbed Ashley resumed his career as a drama critic and wrote regularly for *Theatre Arts*, an American monthly magazine which reviewed theatre from all over the world. His liberal attitude towards theatre was strongly influenced by what he had seen in pre-war Germany and he enthusiastically embraced the expressionist movement of European drama, particularly the work of Reinhardt, Meyerhold and Stanislavsky. He thought that English theatre had become moribund and lazy and consisted of 'stale drawing-room comedy, wearisome intellectual argument, tasteless musical revue or drab detective drama'. He turned to fantasy, creative direction, wordless poetry of theatre, the union of many arts. At first all of this drew him naturally to ballet, but also he delighted in Rambert's love and knowledge of literature. He was less interested in her passion for dance.

Many women of that period sacrificed their own ambitions for making a career once they had married. Not so Rambert, and whilst Ashley provided the climate for her to pursue her interest in dance he was not the first man to be dismayed by his wife's obsession with 'the queer task of training and presenting her dancers'. He accepted that she did not have domestic attributes – and for that matter neither did he – but although he never expected a *hausfrau* he could be forgiven for hoping that once she had children she would give more of her attention to his work and simply treat the dancing as an outlet for her energy. Neither of them was a family person and there is no evidence of family get-togethers, which they agreed were both boring and unproductive. His love affair with ballet eventually ended in disillusionment, particularly with the dancers, whom he considered a silly lot. But in 1919 he was fascinated with his new vivacious wife who shared so many of his own avant-garde views. For her part she admired him, even adored him, but was never in love with him. In some respects she was a typical Polish-Russian woman, there was a puritanical streak in her and although she wished to please her husband she made it plain quite early on that she disliked sex. Ashley was a man who undoubtedly enjoyed the delights of good living and of the flesh. In spite of having so much in common intellectually, time would show that in fact they were not particularly compatible.

And what of Mim's first contacts with her adoptive country? How did she feel on finding herself in the midst of the cool, phlegmatic early twentieth-century English? She was surely perplexed by a tight-lipped society in which nobody lied but nobody told the truth, where emotionalism was left to the masses, where you had to curb your tongue, where you never made 'scenes' either in public or in the home, where an excessive show of affection was met with embarrassment even in private and where politeness often concealed cold hearts and humour was overlaid by a wit that could be cruel. Her spontaneous manner of expressing herself was viewed by her English friends with a mixture of amused disapproval and affection, in fact they treated her as an *enfant terrible*. While they appreciated her mind they shied away from her often boisterous exaggerations. She was to bruise herself many times against these characteristics of her adopted race – and although she was proud to be a British subject she would never really adapt.

It was fortunate for Mim that Enrico Cecchetti, weary of touring with Diaghilev, opened his own school in London in 1918. She returned to her daily lessons while Ashley was still away in Germany. How delighted she was to find the maestro's studio crowded with Russian émigré dancers who had fled the Revolution. Here she renewed her friendships with the dancers of the company who always flocked to his classes whenever they had a season in London. Some of them, including Tamara Karsavina and Lydia Lopokova, married Englishmen and made London their home.

Cecchetti was the greatest teacher of his era and Rambert, a late starter, needed his carefully formulated method of training. This method was precise and allowed no deviation from a meticulously worked-out programme for each day of the week, a sort of menu which produced brilliant, fast footwork, spectacular jumps and beats and a harmonious line of head and arms. He would not tolerate what he called 'acrobatics'. He did not believe in overstretching, nor the exaggerated 'turnout' of the late twentieth century. His method in fact was the foundation stone of English professional training.

Rambert was now bent on learning all she could from Cecchetti and the fanaticism of the classical ballet fan had claimed her. Not to be deterred from her resolution to become a teacher herself, she worked with passion, determined to master at least in her mind if not with her body this most arduous and demanding technique. Poor little Rambert! Try as she would, she simply could not achieve the beautiful arched feet that were the hallmark of the classical dancer. Cecchetti despaired of her. Now in her late twenties she could not alter the shape of her feet and even if she had started training as a child, although she could have improved them with work, those feet were not designed to rise on pointe or perfectly finish the line of an arabesque as if with the stroke of a feather.

With hindsight it is evident that Rambert the teacher took from Cecchetti not only his method of imparting technique but also, unfortunately, his manner of dealing with his pupils. He bullied and insulted them, blissfully unaware that such behaviour would be unacceptable to future generations of dancers. The fiery Italian used colourful epithets to rubbish the work of his earnest English students, who fortunately did not understand his mixture of Italian and bad Russian. Rambert was also to copy his habit of whistling as accompaniment instead of paying for a pianist – an ordeal for the pupils who longed for a good tune to cheer them on the punishing pursuit of perfection. It was just as well that she did not adopt his habit of using a thin malacca cane to guide and prod the bodies of his victims, as he was not above giving them a good whack across the shin to remind them to pull up the muscles of the leg, or to strike the floor with the precision of a metronome if the dancer did not keep time. By the time Mim started to teach the cane had gone out of fashion and it was permissible for the teacher to handle the pupil. Many of her dancers were to remember the painful impact of her index finger jabbing at their shoulder blades.

Cecchetti made a lot of money teaching all day and teaching dances to promising little pupils. But his meanness showed in his refusal to hire a pianist. Nevertheless, when he codified his method his choice of music was excellent, and some of the pieces that accompanied the allegros and adagios were quite beautiful, although musical purists would cavil at his excerpts from Beethoven Sonatas played none too well and permanently lodged in the memory of dancers as a boring accompaniment to difficult exercises over years of training. Set pieces matched each exercise and never varied – a method which suited Rambert with her Eurythmics background.

Among the many English girls who attended Cecchetti's classes was one Irish dancer. Edris Stannus, ten years Mim's junior, was already a seasoned performer in the commercial theatre. She had the qualities of technique that eluded Rambert and was a fine exponent of the Maestro's teaching. She performed under the name of Ninette de Valois and was to join the Diaghilev company in 1923. She would later become a rival and, because of her early and thorough training, would be a thorn in Mim's side who had always felt disadvantaged in this respect.

CHAPTER 8

Ten years were to elapse before Rambert's true destiny was achieved when the Mercury Theatre and, most importantly, the Ballet Club came into being. It was certainly not a dull life, she was not one to stay *sur place* and would never allow life to become humdrum. She filled those years with a variety of theatrical experiences as well as participating in a lively social life with her new husband, continuing her studies with Cecchetti, teaching and involving herself in small experiments which were to help her to mature into what would ultimately be a producer of talent. The dynamo inside herself exhausted everyone around her but they could not help being swept along by her energy and enthusiasm.

Did Ashley Dukes realise the complex nature of this firebrand he had married? Attracted by her charm and vivacity, did he perceive the true woman? Or was he so beguiled by her personality as to be blinded to the passion and intensity of his wife's commitment to dance? He perhaps regarded her obsession as a temporary enthusiasm that would fade away once she produced a family. The dancing kept her occupied and fit and certainly the financial reward of her school would always be useful. Since her pupils were mostly rich upper class this gave them as a couple an entree to pleasant dinner parties given by useful and influential people. Ashley was flattered by the interest shown in his lively wife, he had indeed followed the post-Diaghilev fashion of acquiring fascinating dancers as wives.

As well as her work with Vera Donnet she performed in revues, acted in plays – even playing the role of the French maid in a production of *The Provoked Wife*. She was very proud of this role, going so far as to quote from the text in her autobiography. When in 1921 Diaghilev brought his magnificent but ill-fated full-length production of *The Sleeping Princess* to the Alhambra Theatre Mim haunted the front of house and backstage. Lydia Lopokova wrote, not too kindly, to her husband that 'Mim ran backwards and forwards like a little black beetle.' Rambert was overjoyed to catch up with her former colleagues and, still a stranger in her new country, she found great comfort in the gossip and companionship of dancers of her own background and nationality. She was dismayed by the indifference of the English audiences to a star-studded, sumptuous production such as had never been seen in the West. It is astonishing today to think of those great ballerinas and fine, athletic male dancers performing to the vast emptiness of the Alhambra Theatre.

Rambert, while committing herself to serious daily ballet training, also involved herself with her husband's interests, accompanying him to performances of plays. She, who had transformed herself from the ardent Isadora follower to a chic Parisienne, now went through a third metamorphosis. Ever the performer, she quietened down her image to play the role of wife to an intellectual who was a writer and critic. However, the role of acquiescent wife did not fit her very well, as Ashley was to discover quite soon in the marriage. She was of course interested in the people she met in the world of the artistic milieu of London, and noted with approval that they were more interested in furthering a revival of the arts than of being smart and fashionable, although they would always be happy to name-drop at their dinner parties.

Mim and Ashley were pleased with their first child, although Ashley had not bargained for having to push the pram when Mim went off to her ballet lessons. She had continued training right up to the last minute when Cecchetti, fearful she would give birth in the middle of the *Grand Allegro*, ordered her home. They called the child Angela in celebration of the Armistice and Peace. They had moved to a first-floor flat in a house in Campden Hill Gardens, a pleasant road leading up from Notting Hill Gate. The landlady lived above them and since it was a three-storied house they had to share the entrance and staircase. Shortly after Angela was born they took over another room on the top floor which became their kitchen. There must have been intermittent skirmishes in which the landlady probably came off worse, particularly when her peace was disturbed by the healthy yells of the 'Angel' – and probably Rambert's. When she complained of the noise she received a curt and not very pleasant note from Ashley. She seems to have been gradually elbowed out of the house altogether until it became entirely theirs.

Notting Hill Gate High Street, although even now not particularly attractive, was far less so in the twenties and thirties. A dingy, decaying conglomeration of narrow three-storied buildings huddled together, flats above, shops below, it was a drab thoroughfare sandwiched between the wide stretch of the Bayswater Road with its fine houses and at the lower end the grand sweep of Holland Park Avenue. The local cinema was called the Coronet and had seen grander days. It was originally built as a theatre in 1898 by the same architect who built Wyndham's and the Noël Coward theatres in the West End. If you looked up to its sooty cupola you realised that it was built in the Renaissance style. Ashley Dukes was very taken with the Coronet and mentioned it in his own autobiography. Did he hope to acquire it perhaps? He invested in many properties in the area, but since it still stands now as a cinema it was probably never on offer. If only he had acquired it for a theatre for himself, what a different chapter would have been written in the fortunes of Ballet Rambert.

Mim and Ashley lived their lives in the rarefied atmosphere of the arts. They did not participate in or indeed value the kind of pleasures and diversions of ordinary folk – the cinema, fashionable restaurants, nightclubs, dances or cocktail parties, and they never went to concerts – which is a kind of aberration in their make-up. One wonders how much fun Mim had once she married a husband who was such a highbrow and tended to be intellectually snobbish. Ashley was however a bon viveur, appreciative of good food and wine, but these were tastes that she did not share.

Rambert miscarried her second child, which depressed her to the point when they both decided they did not want any more children. When Mim found herself pregnant again she was furious and blamed Ashley for being 'careless'. They tried to terminate the pregnancy but without success. The child with true Rambert spirit refused to be deterred and turned up on the scene regardless of her parents' wishes. She was given the name of Helena but was always called Lulu, which eventually became simply Lu. Mim, once she'd come to terms with having a second child, wanted a boy. However, once Lulu was born Rambert was enchanted with her. 'Look at my Lu!' she would cry proudly when later her little daughter started to imitate her mother's fondness for turning cartwheels.

Mim met many old friends in Cecchetti's classes. They would always return to their old Maestro whenever there was a London season, she was friendly with Lopokova and adored Karsavina who was a charming, intelligent woman who married Henry Bruce the diplomat and she and Mim became lifelong friends. Not so the English dancer Lydia Sokolova who simply could not stomach Marie Rambert. 'Soky', as she was called, had appreciated Mim's help in *Sacre* but did not accept her claim to teach ballet. An outspoken Englishwoman who spoke Russian fluently she offended Mim on more than one occasion, particularly when she more or less told Mim to shut up at a gala performance at Covent Garden when Mim would not stop talking when the curtain was up. Mim, the great sulker, would not talk to her for some time afterwards.

Sokolova's down-to-earth, thoroughly English no-nonsense personality could not tolerate this 'upstart'. Eight years younger than Mim, she had been born Hilda Munnings in Wanstead, studied with Pavlova, Mordkin and Cecchetti and with her great dramatic gifts became Diaghilev's most spirited, lively dancer. After all she, Lydia Sokolova, had been one of the longest serving members of the Diaghilev company, which gave her an experience far above Rambert's own. She was warm-hearted and generous of spirit but there must have been some resentment from Rambert's side. Axes were temporarily buried when in 1931 Lydia rehearsed the cast for Mim's presentation of *L 'Après-midi d'un faune* with Lydia's husband Leon Woizikovsky dancing the Faune. But she was never invited to either coach or stage a classic at the Ballet Club. However Mim paid her a handsome compliment for her role as the Chosen Maiden in the 1929 revival of *Sacre*. 'She would have made Nijinsky 's heart leap with joy!' she wrote.

In an interview in the sixties for John Drummond's book, *Speaking of Diaghilev*, Sokolova did not mince her words. Rambert's love of exhibitionism was all very well but 'she could not teach the fifth position'. This was unfair and it was tactless of her to voice her opinion, but then tact was not Soky's strong suit. She was mystified as to how, with her limited training and experience, Rambert could found a school which was based on the classical technique. There would be quite a few such negative attitudes in the future but perhaps the people who ran her down failed to understand Rambert's unique qualities.

As well as her contact with the Russian dancers Mim was in almost daily contact with her beloved Vera Donnet, now married to Harold Bowen. Rambert took acting lessons from Vera, who is remembered by Lulu as 'a fat lady to whom she was sent to ascertain whether she, Lu, had any acting talent'. Vera said she did not. In fact she was quite wrong as Lulu could have made a good actress, having inherited her mother's talent in this direction. Lu heartily disliked Vera Bowen who auditioned her for a speaking role but made it plain that she didn't think she was any good. Ashley would have been delighted if his younger daughter had become an actress and would doubtless have helped her in her profession. When she gave up the theatre to marry, he was most disappointed and lost interest in her.

In the twenties the Bowens were socially involved with the Bloomsbury set through Lopokova and her husband, the economist John Maynard Keynes. Rambert did not approve of the Bloomsbury set, their life-style was totally unacceptable to her since she was something of a prude. The Russians and the Poles preserved a high moral tone in matters of sex and Keynes had been firmly told by Harold Bowen that he would have to marry Lydia if he wished to go to bed with her. The Bloomsbury set in their turn did not care for 'Loppy' as she was called, considering that Keynes had married below his own intellectual level. They found her incessant chatter boring, and no doubt behind her back said witty but spiteful things about her. On the occasions when she visited Vanessa Bell's house in Sussex the rest of the entourage would disappear for long walks on the Downs in order to avoid her.

Mim was on the phone every day to Vera, to the irritation of her husband and children, and spent a great deal of time in Vera's house and frequently in town. It was understandable: Vera was a link with the past, they both spoke Russian and belonged to the same culture. As with all émigrés there was a yearning for the language of their past in which they could express themselves freely without the danger of being misunderstood. Loyal as she was to her English family and her new country Mim secretly suffered the special kind of loneliness that émigrés feel, a loneliness that drives them to seek out people of their own land. Sadly, in 1921 Rambert and Vera Bowen fell out. Mim never revealed what the row was about. 'A trivial misunderstanding', Rambert wrote, but however trivial it was enough to stop the two women speaking to each other for several years.

Although still a young woman Mim's character was forming itself increasingly to reveal a nature that could offend and infuriate many of the people around her. She was to become so wrapped up in herself that at times she failed to notice other people's feelings. She expected to be allowed to criticise them but woe betide anyone who dared criticise her, this she would not easily forgive and perhaps that was the problem with Vera.

Rambert gave ballet lessons to private pupils and was gradually collecting the nucleus of a school. In 1920, shortly before Angela was born, she took her exams and got her certificate from Cecchetti and opened her first school in Bedford Gardens. Teaching others is a fruitful method of increasing one's knowledge and she had to take all sorts, many of them not ideally suited to the demands of classical ballet training. But Rambert would not accept a pupil who did not have some quality, even if in some cases it was merely beauty. There is no record of the age group she was teaching but they were probably a mixture of children and teenagers of varied talent. Among these was one interesting boy, Frederick Ashton.

In 1926 Ninette de Valois opened her Academy of Choregraphic Art, a title that Rambert thought 'grandiose and pretentious', nevertheless she had a great respect for de Valois. The curriculum of the new school seemed to embrace everything that she, Rambert, aspired to. Ninette was a formidable rival. She was equipped with intelligence and a thorough knowledge and experience in her profession, having been a soloist in the Diaghilev company. She was ten years younger than Mim, a beautiful woman who had the vision and patience to plan the achievement of that vision – qualities that Rambert lacked. Mim worked by instinct and opportunity but as she herself stated, 'My awful shortcoming is that I cannot look into the future, maybe because I am frightened. I'm an awful coward, unless I get a push I don't move!'

Mim lost all her self-confidence when Ninette announced the opening of her new school. She became depressed to the point where she wanted to give up her own school and send her pupils to Ninette. It must have been a very deep depression, for Ashley threatened to take himself off to America. He had no time for her sulks, being focused on his own career and ambitions. In the event it was the very realisation of those ambitions that saved Mim at the nadir of her life. *The Man With a Load of Mischief* came to her rescue and gave her that much-needed push.

CHAPTER 9

In 1924 Ashley Dukes was writing a play that he had had in mind for some time. *The Man With a Load of Mischief*, a six-handed play set in the Regency period, was 'a neo-Regency comedy of manners'. Set in a wayside inn, it was a mixture of poetic ribaldry and lechery, where the amorous figure of the Prince Regent lurked on the sidelines. The leading stars were Fay Compton and Leon Quartermaine. Presented at the Haymarket Theatre by Nigel Playfair in 1925, it was hailed as a literary triumph and enjoyed a great success, running for eight months – an unusual length for the times.

Mim and Ashley had never lived ostentatiously, they didn't believe in it and both worked hard to earn a living. However, once the royalties from the play came pouring in they might have been forgiven for 'living it up' a bit, but it is doubtful if they changed their lifestyle. They allowed themselves the luxury of hiring a cook and an Irish maid to do the housework, and a nanny for the children. The only perk that Ashley allowed himself was the purchase of a motor car. When, however, he came into the nursery to proudly announce his purchase to Mim and the two girls, Lulu recalls that they all burst into floods of tears!

The money from royalties was put aside towards achieving Ashley's dream of one day owning his own theatre, something that Mim wanted for him too. She of course wanted to participate, but at that time her own ambitions came second to his and besides, she was proud of her husband and went along dutifully with his schemes. In spite of the apparent egotism of this woman she had no idea of her own destiny and that she was the greater of the two neither he nor she knew.

He had his eye on a large hall that belonged to a nonconformist church of the 1850s dominating the corner of Kensington Park Road and Ladbroke Road. Built like the church in Cornish granite in a modern Gothic style, it was the studio of a wood sculptor who used entire treetrunks for his work. It was floored in oak and heavily raftered and once Ashley had acquired it he cut the hall into two sections, one for a future theatre and the other half for a studio. But this was some time ahead. However, it demonstrates that whilst Rambert had no vision for the future her husband certainly had and worked and planned for its achievement.

Around this time Rambert got to know Sophie Fedorovitch, a Russian émigré and a painter who, after escaping from the Revolution had spent some time in Paris painting by day and supporting herself by driving a taxi at night. Rambert had met her at Cecchetti's classes where Sophie would sit and sketch the dancers. A small, mannish woman with a sharp nose and veiled narrow eyes, Fedorovitch spoke in a low growl through barely opened lips. Mim was immediately drawn to this unusual woman, impressed by her intelligence and talent, and there was an instant rapport.

Amongst Rambert's pupils there was a young woman, Frances James, who was interested in becoming a choreographer. Mim was not impressed by her efforts at arranging little ballets for charity performances and took no interest other than allowing her to use her fellow pupils. One day she told Rambert that she wanted to arrange a ballet about a water lily. Mim caught in a bad mood could be almost brutally discouraging but in this instance she showed a polite interest, merely observing that she did not think 'Water Lily' was a suitable name for a ballet. Undaunted, Frances asked her for the French name for 'Water Lily.' *Nénuphar* came the answer and something about the word suddenly kindled Rambert's interest. She talked over the project with Frances and helped with advice and, since Frances had always designed pretty but banal costumes herself, Rambert asked Fedorovitch to do the designs. Sophie produced some lovely costumes which must have delighted Frances albeit finding herself bewildered by Rambert and Sophie chattering away in Russian all through rehearsals. She certainly did not realise that she was participating in a collaboration that would ultimately lead to Fedorovitch becoming one of the great ballet designers of the century.

Sophie sketched the dancers at rehearsal and class and studied the movements closely, understanding that the costume must move with the body and never clutter or obscure the dancer. She got her effects simply with economy of design and when later my mother made costumes for her she was amazed at Sophie's eye for the line and fall of material. This was the first time that Sophie set eyes on the only boy in the class, a skinny young man of eighteen with the mournful face of a romantic poet, large eyes and an aquiline nose, his name was Frederick Ashton. He had begun to train with Léonide Massine who recommended him to Rambert. Long of leg and with beautiful feet, he had no technique to speak of, but he moved with an inborn grace. Physically well co-ordinated, his flowing movements were almost like those of a woman and it was in fact his instinctive understanding of the woman's body that was his greatest achievement as a choreographer.

Mim's School of Russian Ballet was flourishing and when Ashley bought the freehold of Horbury Hall she moved the school from Bedford Gardens to the future home of the Mercury. They gave two very posh cocktail parties to celebrate the opening of the new studio with over a hundred guests at each one. Ashley understood all about influence and promotion and although it may well have been mainly for the furtherance of his own ambition, his support gave Mim a self-confidence that she would not have felt had she been on her own, and she had yet to prove herself. She was cold-shouldered by many of her contemporaries in the 1920s world of ballet, not least by Diaghilev on his visits to London with his Ballets Russes. As she herself writes, he could be charming one moment and ice cold the next.

In spite of the anguished howls that had almost driven Ashley away when Ninette opened her school Mim realised that her own pupils had a special quality which, somewhat to her own surprise, she herself had bestowed upon them. She brought out the Russian style through teaching them variations from *The Sleeping Beauty* and some character dances from the Diaghilev repertory. In 1928 they took part in a charity performance at the Arts Theatre when they danced in the Divertissement which was included in the mixed programme. Sitting out front in the audience Mim saw that her dancers were unlike academic English dancers, they were more expressive and something of the glamour of the Russians had rubbed off on them. While de Valois was visualising a great corps de ballet for her future company Rambert was more interested in bringing out the individual. She would always grumble that Ninette got the best physiques although even in those early days she goaded and bullied her phlegmatic English pupils, she was not interested in cloning and disciplining a row of lookalikes. Although her girls and boys were not all ideal material for classical ballet each one had something of their own to give to dance and she encouraged and brought out their qualities. She saw her pupils as material for choreographers, her classes were not simply to develop them physically, her real aim was to produce interpretative artists and to this end she overlooked technical faults and inadequacies which de Valois would never accept.

On meeting Diaghilev one evening at Covent Garden Rambert invited him to her studio to watch a class. He prevaricated, grandly enumerating the pressure of engagements in his diary. However, probably out of curiosity, he turned up unexpectedly one morning in the middle of the daily class. Mim lost no time in reshuffling the positions of the pupils, placing the best in the front and unceremoniously banishing those she wished to 'hide' to the back – a policy that became a ritual whenever important guests appeared. Later on when she had an additional studio in the basement some poor souls would be ignominiously banished downstairs where they would have to barge into a class in full swing. In these matters Mim was not subtle. She must have been extremely nervous at the sudden appearance of Diaghilev who sat unsmiling and inscrutable on one of the narrow tip-up seats facing the class. He softened a little when he noted that she was teaching the Cecchetti method assiduously. His eye roving through the pupils ignored Ashton, skimmed past William Chappell and Harold Turner (who although an excellent technical dancer Diaghilev considered over muscularised), continued along the line of girls until it came to rest on Diana Gould, tall, long-legged with a beautiful head. After class Mim pressed Diaghilev to watch Ashton's *Leda and the Swan* in which Diana partnered Ashton. Diaghilev was it seems more impressed with Diana's beauty than Fred's choreography but wondered if she would not grow too tall. Mim thought that since she was now sixteen she would not grow any more but she was wrong. However, Diaghilev talked with the starry-eyed Diana and proposed that she should join his company at the end of a further year's training.

Alas, he died before she could do so. She remained with Rambert embittered with disappointment, frustrated that she grew so tall that she was difficult to cast. She always felt that Mim undervalued her and carried a grudge against her that remained for the rest of her life. Rambert herself would always be puzzled by Diana's attitude towards her. 'I don't know what I did wrong', she said, 'I think she did not understand.'

Rambert's pupils arrived having already had a basic training from local teachers. They were dancers who had fallen under the spell of dance at an early age. Mostly the children of well-off parents, they had grown up in an atmosphere of culture and were taken to see performances of Diaghilev, Pavlova and, in the case of Ashton, Isadora Duncan. The inherent English prejudice against male dancers meant that she had plenty of girls but few men. William Chappell, Harold Turner and later Walter Gore and Frank Staff and generations of young men after them received their training free, a lure that was included in her advertisement for the school.

Rambert could burn like a fierce flame at the discovery of a young person of intelligence and talent, listening avidly to their halting words, probing their minds, pulling out of them gifts that they never knew they possessed. Sometimes the recipient of these intense investigations would suddenly find themselves dropped. Having displayed all their wares to the scrutiny of Rambert and basking in the warmth of her interest, she, having found only barren earth under the top soil, would immediately lose interest in her victims and ignore them ever after. When it came to artistic matters Mim was not kind and left behind her a trail of bleeding egos,

Rambert, with Frances James, was now working on a new project originally suggested by Ashley about a famous chef. Since cooking was not a particularly suitable subject for a ballet the chef was changed into a fashionable dress designer, Monsieur Duchic, who, when presenting his beautiful creations to a rapt audience, shocks them when his *pièce de résistance* called *Le Sporran* turns out to be a model dressed in a Scottish sporran. The clientele flee in horror. Monsieur Duchic is disgraced and takes the only way out. He kills himself. Regrettably, Mim who loved to collect 60mm film recordings did not have one of this light-hearted, sophisticated and entertaining little ballet.

Rambert had begun the choreography herself 'aided' by Frances. Ashton was cast in the only male role of Monsieur Duchic. Rambert's choreography was rather scholastic, she never claimed to be a choreographer herself and made a point of differentiating between an arranger of dances – which she was, and a choreographer, a much rarer animal, a point which is often missed. Apart from the fact that Ashton did not have sufficient technique to cope with the complicated enchainements which Rambert and Frances James put together, he plainly did not feel that the steps were right for the role, so 'to the manner born' he invented movements that suited the character perfectly. Rambert immediately perceived that here was an unusual talent and guiding him where he needed help she let him choreograph the entire ballet. It was here that Rambert revealed her genius for discovering talent, and her own lack of conceit. A lesser person would have been annoyed at the temerity of a half-trained student altering the choreography and inventing steps to suit himself and would have replaced him with another dancer (except of course that he was the only man), but Mim could have insisted he toe the line and do as he was told which is the fate of most dancers. He could have stormed out of rehearsal in a huff – even decided he didn't want to be a dancer. It is as well for British ballet that Rambert nurtured and encouraged him at a critical moment in his life.

Nigel Playfair, meeting Rambert socially, asked her about her work and she invited him along to watch a rehearsal. Playfair was impressed, and no doubt to please Ashley who was by now quite famous because of the success of his play, decided to present the ballet in his revue *Riverside Nights* which he was producing at the Lyric Theatre in Hammersmith. The ballet was called *A Tragedy of Fashion*. Rambert as Orchidée, Monsieur Duchic's partner, wore her hair in an Eton crop and smoked a cigar. She first appeared in a gorgeous creation of Fedorovitch, then reappeared in a kilt and the offending sporran. At Playfair's insistence as a final *coup de théâtre* Mim turned cartwheels.

Quite a few people seem to have had a hand in this now historic little *oeuvre*. A.P. Herbert suggested the title and Playfair himself played quite a role in its production. It all sounds a trifle bizarre but it epitomised the slightly crazy atmosphere of the twenties and was a great success, putting Ashton firmly on his future path of choreographer. De Valois rushed round backstage and congratulated Mim on 'finding a real choreographer'. One can only guess at Rambert's thoughts. Did she suspect that even then the clear minded Ninette had plans to filch her discovery?

Mim adored 'her' Fred, he was fun, he was clever and often outrageous. He also was one of the few people in her life who could control her outbursts of temperament and with the intuition of the homosexual understood her anguishes and frustrations. They were great friends and although there might be arguments there were never the furious rows that later on would frequently shake the very foundations of the Mercury.

It was around this time that Rambert was approached by Lilian Baylis who was looking for a teacher-ballet mistress for her actors and drama students at the Old Vic. She offered her the job of a kind of maid of all work, helping the actors and also the office staff (who bolstered up the numbers when necessary) to move well on stage, to arrange dances for plays and operas and offered very little money as recompense. Mim didn't care about the money – she'd have done it for nothing if Baylis had succeeded in firing her enthusiasm, but she didn't.

One has to imagine the meeting of these two formidable women. Rambert, always enslaved by physical beauty, would not have been enamoured of the physical presence of Baylis. Plain faced with a slightly twisted mouth, a legacy from an illness, a clumsy body, dressed in dowdy unfashionable clothes, plain spoken with an obvious lack of wide cultural knowledge, she was the antithesis of everything that Mim admired. Baylis wanted to bring culture to the poor and Rambert was not interested in the poor.

Lilian Baylis, for her part, saw a pushy foreign Jewish woman, fashionably dressed, cryptic in her responses to Baylis's blunt-edged questions. Totally incompatible, the two women parted company. There is no record that they ever met again. Ninette de Valois, however, did rather better and had the vision to seize the opportunity. Rambert turned the job down, Ninette did not. And so the course of English Ballet was set.

By 1928 Mim had an interesting and unusually talented group of students. The glossy and perfect photographs of today's dancers are quite different from the amateurish photography of the early days – there is no comparison. A photograph of a dancer caught in an unfortunate pose, perhaps just about to raise the leg to its full height, perhaps not taut enough, or a foot that has not completed its journey to the fully arched position, will nowadays be ruthlessly thrown out by the ballet master or the dancers themselves. In those more innocent days the photographs, to our sophisticated eyes, are sometimes unkind but they are the only records we have. One taken of the *Pas de Sept* in *Aurora's Wedding* of Madame's pupils has its shortcomings but nevertheless tells us a lot, not only about their personalities but, where the girls are concerned, about their standard. None of them has good feet on pointe except perhaps Diana but the proportions of their bodies are delicate and elegant; none of the men wears tights even though this was in rehearsal. Billy Chappell, the petulant rebel, defiantly wears his outdoor socks, a polo-necked sweater and looks very cross. It is fruitless to compare today's athletically trained dancers to those gentler times when beauty of line and softness of arm and head movement were more important than brilliant technical feats, dazzling pyrotechnics and breathtaking aerial lifts. Most of Rambert's 'boys' in any case were not physically able or indeed willing to hoist the girls higher than shoulder line. The 'Fish dive' and the 'Bluebird' shoulder lift would have reached the limit of what those pretty girls and protesting males were prepared to tolerate. Mim herself adored showing off both of these feats, tiny and as light as a feather she would take a flying leap at one of her men, crying out 'catch me' as she flew. Needless to say not one of them dared drop her – although it must just have crossed Billy Chappell's mind who cavilled at her perpetual nagging to work harder. She considered that although talented he was 'passionately lazy'.

When I was thirteen I was coached by Rambert for the 'Bluebird' pas de deux for a school matinee on the Mercury stage. My partner was Frank Staff, a handsome and strong young dancer newly arrived from South Africa. The rehearsal went well until it came to the final shoulder lift, when the ballerina comes to rest effortlessly on her partner's shoulder in the pose of a bird with its wings (arms) spread, probably quite sensational when first choreographed by Marius Petipa in St Petersburg in 1890. There were no pas de deux classes at the Rambert School in the thirties, merely a rather feeble series of supported pirouettes at the end of a class with a small contingent of weedy cavaliers doing their best with a great many girls. Understandably lifts were not even attempted.

'You do it like this', tiny little Mim who weighed nothing, brightly chirped and without more ado landed on Frank's shoulder fluttering her wings. I stared in horror as Frank gently turned her over and deposited her onto the floor where she took up her pose on one knee.

'Now Breegee – you try it!' She cried enthusiastically. There followed an agonising hour when poor Frank tried to explain what I should do and, terrified, I would hurl myself at him and with a bit of luck land on his shoulder like a sack of potatoes with Rambert screaming at me but offering no practical help whatsoever. The truth of the matter was that she didn't know how to help me since she'd had no experience of double work herself.

Chapter 10

Rambert's pupils had reached a standard where they expected to perform in public and she realised that unless she gave them that opportunity they would drift away – and she was well aware of the predatory nature of de Valois's interest in her activities. Ashton was ambitious and felt he needed experience and received Mim's blessing to join Ida Rubinstein's newly formed company in Paris. Fred had dreams of becoming a *premier danseur* but possessed neither the physical strength nor a taste for the punishing discipline and commitment that this demanded, he was too fun-loving. Massine was dancing and choreographing for Rubinstein and urged his former pupil to take the opportunity of working with what promised to be a most distinguished company. Billy Chappell also joined and he and Fred went off together and in fact stayed for eight months which must have seemed like eight years to Mim struggling to build up her 'Marie Rambert Dancers'.

Ida Rubinstein had been one of Diaghilev's rich amateurs who had joined the company in 1909. She was then twenty-four, old by ballet standards but she was not a classical ballet dancer. She was a member of that band of 'free' dancers inspired by Isadora, known as a 'plastique' dancer, and had also studied acting and mime. Tall, statuesque and a great beauty, she attracted the attention of Fokine who was looking for an artist to portray Cleopatra in the ballet of that name which he was then choreographing. He also chose her for the role of Zobeide in *Schéhérazade* – both character roles.

She left Diaghilev after two years and lived in Paris where she promoted various projects in the theatre, always with herself as the star, and in 1928 she formed a company endeavouring to rival the Diaghilev Ballet. But although she hired the talents of the best of his dancers, composers and designers, Rubinstein was no Diaghilev for she had neither his knowledge nor his impeccable taste. The motivation behind forming such a star-studded company of artists was to create a frame for herself, which suggests that she was one of that vast congregation of *vedettes manquées*. Madame Rubinstein rehearsed in private and when she did make an appearance at rehearsal she was always dressed in magnificent furs, glittering with expensive jewellery, heavily made up and always wearing white gloves.

Miriam Rambam, aged 5.

Ashley Dukes.

The Mercury Theatre.

Auditorium and stage of the theatre.

LYRIC THEATRE
HAMMERSMITH

Sole Lessee and Manager

Telephone : RIVERSIDE 3012

Sir NIGEL PLAYFAIR

A SPECIAL PERFORMANCE

on FRIDAY, MARCH 21st, at 3 p.m. of

The Marie Rambert Dancers

MARIE RAMBERT who will appear as the Madonna in "Our Lady's Juggler"

First Lyric season programme.

Pearl Argyle in *The Lady of Shalott*.

Maude Lloyd and Hugh Laing in *Valentine's Eve*.

William Chappell and Walter Gore in *Façade*.

Holiday snaps

Mim at Dymchurch posing as Taglioni.

Since, perhaps understandably, she didn't like the smell of sweat in the studio the artists were instructed to smother themselves in eau-de-cologne and the men were told to wear clean shirts.

Most of those eight months were spent rehearsing and only a handful of performances given. Fred and Billy had a wonderful time living it up on good salaries and learning a great deal, although it is doubtful whether either of them took the opportunity of taking classes with the famous Russian ballerinas then teaching in Paris: Egorova, Kschessinska and Preobrajenska. They were not fond of class and there was no nagging Mim.

Rubinstein's company became nicknamed 'La compagnie des répétitions'. There was probably quite a lot of sniggering behind closed doors but nonetheless dancers were grateful for the work. She lured the artists by paying well, an important factor, particularly for dancers 'resting' between tours. Diaghilev was at first worried by the emergence of a rival company, but once he had seen a performance he contemptuously dismissed such worries from his mind and wrote a letter to Lifar in which he dubbed the performance, 'provincial, boring and long drawn-out'. 'The corps de ballet was ragged', he went on, 'Nicolaeva pranced about dressed in slime-yellow in a classico-Bacchanalian fashion on her toes, Serge Unger camped it up in a vaguely classical variation in a red wig and green tights and Rubinstein herself appeared as a kind of Pavlova swan, her bodice a mass of false diamonds and wings covered in spangles!' This solo was no doubt the result of many rehearsals with Fokine with whom she had studied in her younger days. He must have come to terms with his pride in return for a well-lined pocket. In spite of Diaghilev's spicy condemnations 'le tout Paris' flocked to the performances and to his indignation actually paid for their seats. The smart dinner tables of fashionable society chewed over a tasty repast of witticisms and ribald laughter as each item in the programme was picked over with wicked relish.

Nonetheless, there was also a great deal for an aspiring choreographer to observe while taking part in works by masters such as Massine, Fokine and Nijinska, and Ashton was intelligent and observant enough to gain the maximum benefit from such an experience. Jean Cocteau was heard to remark, 'It is very useful to look at rubbish – it makes one think.' It certainly couldn't all have been rubbish, not with choreographers of that calibre.

Rambert continued presenting her pupils in various charity performances and galas, working tirelessly to secure engagements and with the help of Ashley making useful contacts and gathering followers who would eventually make up the nucleus of her Sunday night audiences at the Mercury. She still haunted Covent Garden, watching performances by the Diaghilev company, and when she met the great man at a party one evening she was deeply concerned to see how ill he was.

'Where was the giant I had known before?' she wrote. She implored him to take more care of himself and obey his doctors but he simply smiled at her. As with all 'bon viveurs' he found it impossible to do without the good things he had been used to all his life. That was the last time she saw him. One day in 1929 her housekeeper showed her the newspaper announcing his death. In her memoir Mim wrote 'I felt darkness close all around me.' He understood and appreciated the work she was doing as no one else would again and she in her turn understood the temperament of the great man. She would always be faithful to his memory and never ceased to try to capture and hold on to his inspiration with a passion not always shared by her students. Ashton did understand – in a way he would always be her creature.

While *A Tragedy of Fashion* and *Leda and the Swan* had been useful in giving Ashton the chance to draw attention to himself as choreographer, it was the two matinees at the Lyric Theatre in 1930 that attracted favourable notice from both ballet critics and ballet lovers. The performances on February 25 and March 21 were billed as 'The Marie Rambert Dancers'. The unique and distinguished repertoire of the Ballet Club at the Mercury had already begun to flower under Madame's leadership. Not only Ashton but other choreographers were at work. Susan Salaman had come to the school to study dance with a view to becoming a choreographer. She had many ideas but, as with so many novices in the art, she did not realise that dance narrative has to be simple in order to communicate with ease to the public. A complicated narrative is hard to choreograph and Salaman fell into this trap in her first essays, but eventually achieved success with *Our Lady's Juggler*. The ballet was based on a mediaeval legend about a poor juggler who on a saint's day is a bystander watching gifts being laid at the feet of the statue of the Virgin Mary. Having nothing to give he horrifies the crowd by performing tricks, ending up with a handstand as his homage to her. Salaman caught the period perfectly, designing the costumes in collaboration with her brother Michael and devising rustic semi-character steps for the villagers and expressive movements for the acolytes bringing their offerings. Whatever economies Ashley Dukes may have made in the equipping of his theatre, he did not stint on the lighting equipment which was excellent and made a great contribution to the presentations.

This was one of the first ballets in which I was allowed to appear in 1935 on the Ballet Club stage as a gawping fourteen-year-old rustic. The most fascinating feature of this ballet was the participation of Mim herself as the statue of the Virgin Mary. I have a vivid memory of her looking quite beautiful wearing a long dark blue robe and a recreation of Vera Donnet's wonderful make-up that she had devised for *Pomme d' or*. She stood on a pedestal against a sky-blue backcloth quite still, her eyes lifted to heaven for the entire ballet. From time to time I peeped over my shoulder to see if she moved, but she did not seem even to blink, a great feat of discipline for someone so lively. At the end of the juggler's dance, when he stood at the foot of the pedestal in homage, she slowly moved her hand in which she held a veil and gently dropped it over the juggler's bowed head. It was a wonderful *coup de théâtre*. It was the only time I saw Rambert perform as by that time she had given up participating in performances and gave all her time and energy to producing her artists. But this particular role was I think dear to her and since she was deeply religious had a special significance.

Another new ballet by Ashton was his *Capriol Suite*; a sequence of sixteenth-century dances to Peter Warlock's score based on music from Arbeau's *Orchésographie*. Although perfectly within the manner of Elizabethan formal dances Ashton succeeded in interpreting the style with taste and originality. It lasted only ten minutes, so ranked as a 'divertissement' rather then a ballet and it was a perfect cameo featuring Diana as the beautiful centrepiece between her two partners Ashton and Chappell. It was recreated by the Rambert Dance Company in 1984 and continues to be regarded as a seminal work that will never date.The costumes were designed by Billy Chappell, who was allowed in true Rambert fashion a miserable sum of money to produce three voluminous period costumes in what should have been rich silks and velvets. He solved the problem by raiding Pontings' bargain basement with Mim in tow tightly clutching her purse strings. They bought a large roll of unbleached calico at sixpence a yard, and Billy washed and dyed it, then painted it so that under clever lighting the costumes looked like the real thing. The lack of funds of the early Rambert ballets drew out of the designers a resourcefulness of imagination and creativity which might not have surfaced had they been given the large budgets of today's designers.

The programme for the two matinees was a generous one. Besides *Juggler* and *Capriol*, it included some dances which Ashton had arranged for a production of Purcell's *The Fairy Queen*, and *Mars and Venus,* a little ballet which Fred had arranged to Scarlatti music chosen by Mim. She was tireless in searching out music and themes to inspire her choreographers and although at times her total involvement wearied and irritated her protégés there is no doubt that Fred and his successors gained enormously from her knowledge and a practical eye for what worked in theatrical terms.

Also included in the performances were excerpts from *Aurora's Wedding*. This was a one-act adaptation from Diaghilev's star-studded production, presented in the disastrous season at the Alhambra Theatre in 1921. Legions of Madame's pupils were to struggle through these technically difficult variations drawn from the prologue and the final act of the ballet which she always taught at the end of the children's afternoon classes at the Mercury in the thirties. She never strayed far from the ultimate goal of all training – to produce dancers capable of becoming professionals. She was way ahead of her time in this philosophy and it was a tradition that was born at the Lyric matinees when the founding members of the Rambert company gave their first performances under the critical eyes of critics and ballet lovers.

It was perhaps during the rehearsals for these exacting solos, pas de trois and pas de deux that her pupils discovered for the first time the full force of her famous bullying tactics. These tactics consisted of a mixture of coaxing, pleading and colourful verbal abuse that sometimes reached a crescendo of indignant hooting, anguished howls and shrieks of disgust. The reactions of her pupils were commensurate with their temperaments and Mim's verbal attacks commensurate with their abilities. The calm beauty of Pearl Argyle bedazzled Mim who treated her almost with adulation, and although Pearl did not possess a strong technique her beauty of face and form and the intelligence of her approach to her work silenced criticism and corrections were proffered in a velvet glove. She was perfect for the intimacy of the Ballet Club stage but, as with many of her colleagues, she lacked the ability to project in a large theatre where weakness of technique was more noticeable.

Diana Gould on the other hand provoked pithy comments on her work which were sharply returned by Diana, who had as good if not a better command of the English language and certainly as sharp a wit. It was Diana's misfortune that she grew so tall. Rambert had always hated tall people, she literally felt dwarfed by them. None of her company was more than five-foot-two, Suzette Morfield was a favourite at five feet. A sweet-faced, gentle girl, she never provoked Rambert who had trained her from the beginning. Too much heavy barre-work (one of Mim's failings,) had developed over-muscular legs, but Suzette had a charming personality and was perfectly suited to the role of the little milkmaid in the original production of Ashton's *Façade* and as Little Red Riding Hood in the *Aurora* divertissement. When she gave up dancing she took up nursing, rising to the status of matron. The capacity for dedication in ballet training has a parallel in nursing and religion and there have always been cases of dancers, once they have given up their careers, finding fulfilment in these occupations. Gillian Martlew, a distinguished member of the Rambert company in the fifties and early sixties, later became a nun.

Andrée Howard was an ideal Rambert dancer, small-boned with a light quality, again no great technician, none of them was, but she was a creative artist. She possessed the golden-red hair, the high forehead, the large pale eyes, and the rather long nose of a Flemish painting, and indeed she was an adopted child of Belgian origin. She was that rare thing, an exceptionally gifted woman choreographer. She could sculpt, paint, design, make her own clothes, and in the early days of the Ballet Club made some of the costumes for her own ballets. Highly imaginative, a perfectionist, she was not easy to work with and there was something plaintive about her personality, a deep unhappiness and restlessness that culminated later in the 1960s in a tragic death.

Prudence Hyman was the strongest dancer amongst Mim's pupils and Arnold Haskell, the critic, prophesied stardom for her. However, Pru abandoned the ballet to 'go commercial'. Unlike her fellow pupils who all came from well-off families, Pru had to earn her living from her dancing. Elisabeth Schooling, another of the original Rambert dancers, was the most vulnerable of Mim's pupils. At fourteen she had auditioned for Rambert who admired her feet but would always complain of what she called Elisabeth's 'woolly' legs. A sensitive girl, she suffered the most from Mim's wounding expletives and invariably ended up in tears.

Maude Lloyd, another distinguished pupil, came to Rambert in 1927 and was the first of a series of dancers from South Africa (Pearl was another). Maude's family in Cape Town was not well off and her teacher Helen Webb had raised a fund to send her to England and continue her studies with Rambert. Maude was a fine-boned, elegant dancer, timid of disposition but never intimidated by Mim who took her under her wing and saw to it that she was properly housed and fed. This was the paradox of Rambert; the kind woman who was sympathetic to her dancers' personal problems and difficulties, who almost cosseted them, but spared them no quarter when it came to the standard of their work.

Mim was more careful of the men who if pushed too far would give her as good as she gave. Ashton she treated as an equal, he was a friend and she treasured him. Nevertheless, he too could come in for mild, if amusing, abuse as on the day in class when she shouted 'Freddy! stop waving your bottom about like a banner!' He appreciated her wit although not everybody did. Billy Chappell certainly had plenty of wit, but perhaps not of Mim's sort. He was a gentle, indolent soul with none of Fred's ambition and for whom the pursuit of technique was an arduous and painful experience which he was not quite convinced was necessary. He had initially studied art and became a brilliant designer but was not a choreographer, although perfectly capable of arranging dances for musical theatre and revues later in his career. One suspects that his heart was not really into ballet and he certainly resented Mim's teaching methods and objected to the often humiliating invectives that came rolling irresistibly like a torrent off Rambert's tongue. He was, however, fond of her and appreciated her qualities. He was physically beautiful and very clever. Perhaps he suffered from being in Fred's shadow, they were great friends although it was never a relationship. It is not surprising that he later turned to the broader theatre to become a most successful director of serious plays and revues. He eventually deserted Mim to join the Vic-Wells Ballet and seems to have found greater compatibility with de Valois. He stayed with the company for several years and designed many of the ballets.

No ballet company worthy of the name can dispense with a virile male dancer equipped with the technique to cope with the demands of classical roles. Such a one was Harold Turner. A north country boy, at nineteen he was already well trained when he came to London. Not a typical Rambert product, having neither the intellect nor the creative talent of some of his colleagues, he was nevertheless a valuable asset being a strong dancer possessing a good elevation, brilliant pirouettes and beats and being a good strong partner. He partnered Pru Hyman in *Bluebird pas de deux*, coping effortlessly with the complicated beats and *tours en l'air*, and taking the part of Harlequin to Karsavina's enchanting Columbine in Fokine's *Carnaval* which was added to the programme for the second season. He later graduated to the Vic-Wells company and I have a vivid memory of Turner in *Les Patineurs* performing a seemingly endless series of *grandes pirouettes à la seconde* centre stage while the curtain descended slowly on a twirling, shimmering snowstorm, surely one of Ashton's happiest inspirations.

Rambert's dancers were ideally suited to *Carnaval*, a delightful ballet to Schumann's music. Diana was perfectly cast as Chiarina, Andrée with her lightness of movement was a natural Papillon and Billy was the embodiment of the lugubrious clown, Pierrot, endlessly and hopelessly pursuing Columbine. Notable in this production was the casting of Mim herself as Estrella. She crammed those unsuitable feet into pointe shoes and got away with it on sheer personality.

These were the main components of those first seasons at the Lyric of the Marie Rambert Dancers. It was the very diversity of personality and character of those early Rambert dancers that was so interesting. No stony-faced corps de ballet here, although the girls were perfectly capable of moulding themselves into an integrated group when required. The choreographers found this very diversity inspiring and devised roles for them that suited their individual qualities and masked their shortcomings. How lucky they were! Did they realise that it is every dancer's dream to have a role specially created for them? To be cast in a role for which they felt sympathy and in which they could express themselves fully? Of course this did not happen for all the dancers but they were there in the rehearsal room taking part and witnessing the birth pangs of hesitant, nervous young choreographers trying out their ideas, agonising over eight bars of movement and encouraged by Rambert, the 'midwife', as she has been dubbed. And this was when Mim was at her best, happy, engrossed, quiet in her concentration and avid in her support and interest. This was what she was all about. Teaching was what she had to do and she did it conscientiously and to the best of her ability.

Classes were one thing, but now with the Lyric season she was putting her professional reputation on the line. It mattered desperately to her and with her inexhaustible energy she nagged like a terrier drawing out of those phlegmatic, cool, slightly detached English students an approach that was essentially Russian in manner and style. Did she realise her own courage? She said many times in her life that she was a coward, but at a period when after Diaghilev's death ballet had lost its interest in England she had the courage, some would say the nerve, to present a whole evening of ballet to a sceptical public. No one else was doing it. She had seen and taken part in the greatest company the world had ever seen, and somehow she wanted to keep that memory alive no matter how modest her contribution.

Her efforts were amply rewarded by the success of the Lyric matinees, which led to Playfair offering Rambert a fortnight's season. The only stipulation he made was that there must be a star and suggested Tamara Karsavina should be approached. Mim for all her swagger had a genuine humility in regard to great artists and no more so than for her adored Karsavina. How could she with her humble group of inexperienced pupils ask Karsavina to dance on the same stage? She did go and see Karsavina 'in fear and trembling'. That gracious lady, perhaps admiring Mim's passionate enthusiasm, proposed that she should mount *Les Sylphides* and dance the leading role. At the age of forty-five she was still slim and beautiful and for Mim's little group of fledgling dancers it must have been an unforgettable experience.

The stereotype image of a ballerina by her fellow dancers is not particularly sympathetic. She is regarded as remote, snooty, possessing an elevated opinion of herself, aided and abetted by the hysterical adoring aficionados who cluster outside the stage door and for whom she represents a cross between a film star and a goddess, the kind of adulation accorded to today's footballers and pop singers. Mim, while appreciating the talents of these ladies, could find nothing interesting in them as people. Karsavina was the exception. A cultured and highly intelligent woman, she had been adored by Diaghilev who, it is said, had he not been a homosexual would surely have married her. She was the personification of the greatest days of the Maryinsky, about which she had written so beautifully and skilfully in *Theatre Street* just published in 1930. One can imagine those students at the end of the day, worn out, feet up, avidly reading the book and basking in the reflected glory of those magical years of Karsavina's training at the greatest school in the world and her subsequent career. Those awe-struck young dancers loved her on sight and found her an inspiration, gently coaching them in the style of Fokine's evocation of nineteenth-century romanticism. Who else could have given them this opportunity at that time? Only Marie Rambert. Ashton partnered Karsavina, modest and self-effacing, and what he may have lacked in elevation and technique he amply compensated for by his image of the pale romantic poet. This production of *Les Sylphides* by Karsavina was faithfully treasured by Mim throughout the lifetime of the original Ballet Rambert.

The Lyric season was so successful that it led to two more seasons, during which time the company was joined by Leon Woizikovsky and Sokolova,who must by then have revised her original prejudices about Rambert. Both these dancers were fine artists who but for the death of Diaghilev would surely not have been interested in Mim's little venture. 'Pan Leon', as he was called. was a delightful, dynamic Pole whose working companionship gave Mim enormous pleasure. Sokolova had danced in the original Diaghilev production of *L'Après-midi d'un faune* and coached the nymphs in the difficult choreography and music. Again, this was a seminal production, to be later reproduced for Nureyev by Elisabeth Schooling who was one of the nymphs and who possessed a prodigious memory for many of the original Rambert productions.

What of Mim herself? Teachers as a rule suffer agonies of doubt about their classes, about their students, about themselves. They worry as to whether they have handled situations in the right way, should they have said so-and-so? Was the student right? Did they give a good class? Those were more autocratic days. As a student said to me in the 1960s, 'This is the last bastion of authoritarianism – fascinating!' Was she really a teacher? Not in the strictest meaning of the word, for she did not have the patience nor indeed the time (she was already thirty-two) for the plodding boredom of constantly repeated exercises, although she was punctilious in giving these in the Cecchetti manner. It is doubtful whether Mim was worried or had sleepless nights. She felt that since her students wanted to be good dancers, good artists, they must simply accept whatever means she felt she had to use to meet that end. Besides, that was what she herself had witnessed, it was the way it was. Recognising that she was dealing with, in comparison to the Diaghilev dancers, limited talent, facility and physiques, she was doing whatever was needed to draw out from her dancers their maximum abilities. She took it for granted that it was an undeclared pact. They came to her to help them realise their potential, she on her part was prepared to give them every ounce of her energy and knowledge. That being a foreigner, unused to the ambiguousness of the English language, she expressed herself in colourful and not particularly tactful words was part and parcel of the excitement of being involved in a unique experience. They were happy to endure the shafts of wit at their expense that could sometimes be hilariously funny.

There were three seasons in all at the Lyric Hammersmith and they established Marie Rambert as a force in the birth of British ballet which took precedence at the time to Ninette de Valois's enterprises in Rosebery Avenue.

CHAPTER 11

It was not until I returned to the Mercury as a teacher in the late 1950s that I fully appreciated the standard of workmanship that had gone into the creation of the theatre. When as a child in 1935 I joined the afternoon children's class I took such things for granted. I was more fascinated by Madame's studio next door with its huge oak beams straddling the vaulted ceiling, the numerous gothic doors leading from the studio, behind one of which we changed shivering from cold in winter. Most of all I was hypnotised by the little bird-like lady with the piercing black eyes who spoke to me in French and called me 'Breegee'.

It was only later that I noticed the quality of the heavy oak double doors at the entrance of the building and also into the auditorium, the brass fittings now dulled with time but which then shone like burnished gold, the original paint work still there albeit pock-marked and chipped from the imprint of hundreds of young fingers. The awful emergency exit doors, heavy and cross-barred with drop rods that scraped noisily across concrete when pushed open – that is if you knew the secret of those levers which required a brutal assault to get them to move. The conversion from hall to theatre took place at a time when real materials were employed and the workmanship a matter of pride rather than expediency. The parquet flooring in the green room, the solidity of the long bar behind which Ashley Dukes the omnipotent mine host served wine, beaming on the customers, all bore the test of time and were made to last.

The stage, that minuscule space measuring eighteen by eighteen feet, was solidly built. You could leap and crash and fall on that imperturbable surface with confidence. The three rounded steps that led down from the apron stage into the auditorium were equally safe and solid and the walls against which you crashed as you made your spectacular exit into narrow wings could certainly knock you out if you overshot your *grand jeté*. The doors on either side of the proscenium opening were real doors and the two corpulent gilded cupids that hovered over them had flown all the way from Venice. The long tapestries that hung from the walls of the auditorium were genuine too, not to mention the splendid chandelier casting a gentle light over the yellow-plushed 150 seats. The atmosphere was of a private theatre in a grand country house, exclusive, unashamedly elitist.

There was just enough room between the front seats and the stage to accommodate a grand piano at which sat Charles Lynch, a tall thin man of Dickensian appearance. Angus Morrison was to join him later when another piano was installed.

Ashley Dukes enjoyed acquiring property and was good at it. Not only did he acquire the two houses adjacent to the original hall, but during the thirties several houses in the locality and, oddly, the local fire station (after it had ceased to function as such). Most importantly he bought a parade of shops just a short walk along from the Mercury and also the piece of land behind with cottages and stables which were later demolished leaving space for what was planned to be the new, larger theatre. Plans were drawn up and I recall seeing sketches of the new Mercury in the newspaper at various intervals. What a splendid vision! How exciting! A theatre at the corner of Ladbroke Road, and how necessary to that part of London which has always attracted people from all branches of the arts. But after several years had passed there was no new Mercury. In 1940 he wrote in his autobiography, 'I ought of course to have run about London to look for somebody to buy this property for me and then have persuaded him to build the theatre.' There is something poignant about the epitaph to his unfulfilled dream, 'This ruinous and weed-grown patch of London soil is the visible monument (I will not say graveyard) of hopes aroused by dramatic poets in the late 1930s.'

The strength and weakness of Mim and Ashley lay in the fact that they wanted complete autonomy over their enterprises, an understandable wish since they could then keep control over the artistic standards they set themselves. But they did not have the money themselves and he relied on mortgages and bank loans. There were no guarantors, no committee. They did not want to share. Their pride, some might say their arrogance, would not allow them to 'go around with a begging bowl', as Mim put it. When later she was forced to accept financial help to keep her company afloat it was a most disillusioning experience for her. They were both autocrats, it was a family affair and they resented what would be the inevitable interference from enthusiastic rich amateurs who in return for their support would expect to have their say in the artistic policy of the theatre.

However, they did listen to the advice of Arnold Haskell who had become an avid fan of Rambert during the Lyric seasons, recognising the value of the work she was doing. In the early thirties he was on his way to becoming an eminent critic and when the Ballet Club was founded he became a director. He was uninhibited about voicing his opinions and he was knowledgeable, something that Mim, no respecter of critics, appreciated.

A lively little man with bright intelligent eyes and a receding chin, later to be concealed beneath a scholarly black beard, he adored the Russian dancers and found the English obsession with the almost mathematical importance of precision arid and unexpressive. He admired Rambert's encouragement of dance drama and found her dancers 'of marked individuality and not simply the competent performers of classroom steps'. He darted about excitedly as much as Rambert herself, tending to go overboard for his favourite ballerina or promising newcomer. He invented the word 'balletomania' which perfectly described the kind of manic obsession that could strike ballet enthusiasts. He himself never missed a performance and haunted backstage, although at the Mercury there was certainly no room for Arnold in the wings.

The little theatre in Ladbroke Road was originally called the Ballet Club when it opened in 1931, being registered as a club theatre and being only 'semi public'. Judging by the design of the stage it is clear that Ashley was creating a place for the fulfilment of his own projects in drama without taking too much account of the suitability of the stage for dance. One wonders whether there were arguments at home with Mim fighting her corner? It's doubtful, she was so grateful for his help and support in so many other respects that she made the best of the resources available. In Ashley's mind the ballet came second, he never really liked the dancers whom he thought a silly lot and privately disapproved of homosexuals. However, the revenue that his wife brought in from her school provided an invaluable subsidy for his projects.

At first the company put on short seasons of ballet but these were not successful. Besides not attracting a large enough audience the artists were not always available during the week, they received no salaries and had to earn their living working in musicals and of course the best of them – Ashton, Chappell, Argyle – for Ninette de Valois, a sore point with Mim who could not offer them a professional theatre. So finally it was decided to settle for Sunday night performances and they soon gathered an enthusiastic following from the ballet world and from influential 'names' in society.

The performances started at nine. Ashley looked after front of house, which he thoroughly enjoyed, seeing to the printing of the programmes, in which he was listed as the director trading under the title of 'Nameless Theatre, Ltd.', and customers were firmly bidden to park down the middle of Kensington Park Road round the corner. He even took the trouble to print a fragment of map to help people find the Mercury. When my mother and I started to attend the performances in 1933 the box-office was a tiny

'Wendy House' in the foyer of what had been the entrance hall of the house next to the Mercury. There were heavy double doors which led one into the drawing-room of the next house which had become the greenroom, the walls of which were lined with original lithographs of romantic nineteenth-century dancers, a unique collection gathered lovingly by Ashley and which spent many years after Rambert's death in the vaults of the Victoria & Albert Museum. This room, having been knocked through, now accommodated the long bar.

The programmes were yellow ochre in colour, the print a distinctive dark blue, the paper of such a quality that the programme is still intact and perfectly readable after sixty years. In just two pages, the contents were set out with accuracy and taste, no photographs, no profiles of the artistes, the only advertising being for productions in which Dukes himself was involved, also the *Theatre Arts Monthly* (to which he contributed articles), and information about membership of the Ballet Club; ten shillings yearly, life membership fifty shillings. The accents of the audience were unashamedly upper class and if any members of the lower orders innocently wandered into the performance they kept their mouths firmly shut.

Ashley and Mim made a good team. She was responsible for backstage, he for the front of house. At performances Mim was at her most delightful, chatting up important people, urging the society ladies to yield up their fabulous discarded Schiaparelli and Worth evening dresses to her wardrobe to be remade into costumes for the ballets, also canvassing for pupils for her school. She was the best PR woman the Rambert Ballet ever had – not least for her utter loyalty to her company whatever private misgivings she may have had. She spent a lot of that inexhaustible energy scuttling backwards and forwards through the pass door between the auditorium and the studio galvanising her brood into more action, getting under their feet, often upsetting them by some unfortunate reference to their make-up or appearance.

There was some stage-management although the general staging and lighting of their ballets was organised by the choreographers themselves, the male dancers doubling as electricians and stage-hands. The props and scenery made on the premises were of the flimsiest variety but worked well enough although woe betide the dancer who inadvertently knocked something over on a hasty entrance or exit.

There was no room at all behind the stage once the backcloth was in place, dancers had to enter from the same side they exited. If by some misfortune they got it wrong the scramble behind the backcloth made it ripple and sway, whereupon Mim would throw herself through the pass-door like a bat out of hell and indulge in furious and vociferous scolding quite clearly heard by the audience. There was a staircase centre back leading up to a dressing-room which ascended sideways straight off the stage. This also required good planning on the part of the senior dancers who used it. There was only one toilet backstage and that was downstairs so visits had to be strictly rationed to the intervals. Whatever the crisis the artists had to talk (or swear) in whispers as the audience could hear everything that was going on. Mim, however, exerted some licence in that respect, hissing loudly at a poor unfortunate girl from behind the blue velvet curtain (lined with yellow satin) which was the wing.

When the Ballet Club first opened the studio served as box office and greenroom. This must have thrilled the audience since the dancers in costume and make-up also had to pass through to get to the dressing-rooms and the stage. Ballet has about it an aura of strangeness, almost enchantment, probably because it is so unattainable to the ordinary man and woman and fascinates its followers into a kind of awed reverence. One might think that with such close proximity to the audience in that tiny theatre this ambience would be lost, but not so and I can still feel a frisson of magic recalling the evenings when my mother and I sat in the audience for those early performances. We were certainly as much, if not more enthralled than at performances of the Vic-Wells Ballet in Rosebery Avenue.

All-in-all it was a hands-on affair and none the worse for that. It gave fresh young artists a sense of responsibility and resourcefulness and in those early days of English ballet the excitement of the discovery of the new. She who had instigated and inspired the whole thing would for quite a few years find herself pushed aside, almost forgotten until the fifties when she received the CBE, the first of many recognitions. It is astonishing to realise what was accomplished in that tiny theatre and on such a basically unsuitable stage. Ironically it is Ashley Dukes's contribution which has been forgotten.

CHAPTER 12

My first taste of Marmite sandwiches was in 1933 when at the age of twelve I was invited back to tea at Campden Hill Gardens. I sat at the table in the rather sombre dining-room with the whole family, Rambert, Ashley, his sister Irene and the two girls, Angela and Lulu. A shy child, I felt intimidated to find myself amongst such an awesome family gathering.

I viewed Ashley with apprehension, I don't know why, he seemed affable enough sitting at the head of the table like a Victorian paterfamilias. I did not think him handsome; he had the flushed face of the bon viveur and looked much too large in comparison to his wife, sister and two daughters all of whom were quite thin. His presence conveyed a general air of superiority and he exuded a condescending benevolence that I found vaguely unpleasant. I don't remember what they talked about, I was tongue-tied and although I was never frightened of Rambert I felt ill at ease at the sight of my charismatic teacher munching Marmite sandwiches across the table from me. There was none of the easy familiarity, the free inconsequential talk of the average family, but then this was not an average family. Lulu later confided she was in awe of her father as a child and blushed whenever he addressed her at table. I myself was always to feel when talking to Rambert that I must never say anything that was pointless or faintly stupid and even at twelve I picked up on the strained atmosphere of the house. The Marmite sandwiches were, however, a great discovery.

Ashley must have found marriage to this turbulent soul wearying. Her outbursts of unrestrained fury were dealt with in the only possible way, amused tolerance, which of course infuriated her the more. One of many scenes at the family lunch table came to a climax when Mim made a dramatic exit carrying her plate of food, knife and fork and sat eating it on the front doorstep of the house. It was a frequent occurrence, it seems she enjoyed sitting on the doorstep since there was no garden. This must have fascinated the people living opposite. On such occasions Ashley would comment to the children sitting sheepishly over their plates, 'Your mother's having one of her turns', an expression he'd overheard from one of the maids. These 'turns' invariably ended up with Mim retiring to her bed with one of her migraines, sometimes for days.

But the children were fond of him and to a certain extent sympathised with him regarding their mother. It was Mim who was unhappy, A sulker, she sometimes didn't talk to Ashley for days. 'Your mother's gone silent', he would remark to the girls and they learnt to take it in their stride. The two Irish maids were always threatening to leave, but Mim often ended up crying in the kitchen, going back to her childhood when she would take refuge in the kitchen in her native land. The Irish maids of Campden Hill Gardens were to have a great influence on her religion and through them she found her way back to becoming a devout Catholic. Ashley, though, was anti-religion, and that must have been painful for Mim.

When asked by a friend whether he felt hen-pecked by all these women in his house Ashley retorted, 'I am not hen-pecked – I am the hen-pecker!' He was quite happy and went about his life in his own way but his love of 'putting himself amongst the ladies' became an increasing thorn in Mim's side. He went to America with *The Man with a Load of Mischief* in 1924 and on his return unwisely revealed to Mim that he'd had an affair. Whatever was he thinking of to make such a confession? She wasn't one of the liberal-minded Bloomsbury set with their theories of sexual freedom. Rambert's Eastern European origins, coupled with a puritanical, almost Victorian attitude to sex, should have warned him of her predictable reaction. She could not forgive him and, deeply hurt, she banished him from her bed.

Mim had no interest in home-making as her home was the dance studio. She never had to cook, sew, clean or do washing and ironing because there were always domestics to do that, right back into her childhood. She was useless in practical matters and had not a vestige of business sense. At the same time she was spartan in her attitude to the comforts of life. Both Angela and Lulu were to become devoted wives, which Mim could not understand. 'My daughters have both become slaves to their husbands', she complained. Although she adored Ashley and suffered great jealousy of other women in his life she was certainly not prepared to turn herself into a slave.

After hiring a succession of unsatisfactory nurses and governesses, the last one was fired for leaving Angela alone in the house, Ashley's unmarried sister Irene came to live with them and virtually brought the girls up. There was some mystery about Renee, as she was called. She had suffered a nervous breakdown. As a girl she had been a brilliant scholar, immensely clever, matriculated with a first and had wanted to go on to Oxford. However, her Baptist clergyman father decided it would be a waste of much-needed money.

There were three sons to educate, and one of Ashley's brothers, Sir Paul Dukes, was a most unusual and chameleon-like personality. He lived in St Petersburg in 1909 where he studied the piano at the Music Conservatoire. He spoke fluent Russian and had fallen under the spell of the ballet at the Maryinsky at performances attended by the Tsar and his family. He was knighted for his work for the secret service in Soviet Russia. A follower of Peter Ouspensky, the Russian occultist, Dukes was a bit of a crank, dabbling not only in the occult, but also in fasting and Yoga. He flirted with herbal elixirs, played the piano brilliantly, composed discordant music, had learnt acrobatics and tap dancing and on meeting Nicholas Legat, the great teacher from the Imperial Theatres, determined to learn to dance. He joined Legat's classes, wagering that although he was in his late thirties he would master the classical technique. Legat, struggling to build up a school in London in the late twenties, was only too glad to get another paying pupil no matter how unsuitable that pupil may have been. Actually Paul seems to have had a reasonable facility and was fascinated by Legat and particularly by his fiery younger wife, Nadine Nicolaeva. He became her lover, a situation sadly accepted by her husband, and Paul became part of the ménage. Unpredictable, regarded by Legat as a rich dilettante, he disappeared from time to time on his secret business and after a while would suddenly reappear in class. He trained intermittently for three years and being supple and extremely intelligent made rapid progress. Along with the flamboyant Nicolaeva as his partner he was coached by Legat in the spectacular aerial lifts already known in Russia but not in the the west.

Most bizarre of all, this extraordinary man adopted the stage name (could it have been his cover?) of Paul Dukaine and formed an acrobatic act with Nadine and another Russian, Serge Renoff, which toured the music halls of England for some time until he finally got bored and drifted away. In 1932 he translated Legat's book, *The Story of the Russian School*, from the Russian and paid for it to be published.

What did Rambert and Ashley think of this strange, unpredictable member of the family? Surely if he was so interested in ballet his place should have been alongside them? Nicholas Legat and Rambert loathed each other. He regarded her as a balletic parvenue, and although she accepted that he was a great teacher she considered that Nicolaeva was a vulgar exhibitionist. It's probable that Paul suggested he join her classes and she told him bluntly that he was too old. However, in spite of his defection to the Legats he seems to have remained on good terms with his sister-in-law.

It is not known whether it was the dashing of her hopes for an academic career that unstabilised Renee, or perhaps it was the loss of a fiancé in the First World War. Those were still the days when a woman had to justify her existence by marrying and having children. For a time she was incarcerated in a mental institution and it was after this that she came to Campden Hill Gardens, giving up her chance of a private life by devoting herself to the family until the forties when sadly she again had to be put away. Not only did she educate and care for the girls, she ran the house, became Mim's secretary and attended to many of the countless chores that arose from the growth of the school. There was a strangeness in her personality difficult to define. Spinsters were the butt of jokes in those days and she was certainly typical of the breed; prudish, unworldly and hated men. I can still see this tall, thin lady hovering in the background of our afternoon children's classes, emanating the same kind of lofty superiority as her brother and conducting prospective parents round the premises extolling the virtues of Rambert and emphasising the refinement of the type of pupil who entered the portals of the school.

Mim on marrying Ashley had been told firmly never to mention that she was Jewish, a ridiculous bit of prejudice that in any case was futile, everyone knew she was and Renee revealed in a moment of confidence to my mother that Mim's father had been a rabbi. This information has never been substantiated although there was a dynasty of rabbis in Poland with the name of Rambam in the fifteenth century. It was perhaps one of Renee's snobbish fairy stories to build up Mim. There were two titled girls training at the school, Lady Rose Paget and Lady Daphne Finch-Hatton. Shortly after Daphne's marriage to Witney Straight my mother overheard Renee on one of her prospective parents' tours tell the awstruck couple that 'We have quite a few members of the aristocracy training here, Lady Daphne Finch-Hatton, Lady Rose Paget and of course Lady Straight.' Angela and Lulu were not told of their Jewish blood until they were in their teens. It seems incredible that there had been no inkling of Rambert's origins within her own family for so many years or indeed that it had been necessary to keep silent. As it was it was a shock to the girls and upon finally receiving this piece of information they cried all night! 'We left it too late', Rambert admitted later in her life.

Family holidays were spent in Dymchurch where Ashley rented a property that had been converted from army barracks in the First World War. Dymchuch, an old smuggling port, is famous for its Romney, Hythe and Dymchurch Railway and boasts a Martello tower and vast stretches of sandy beaches. Now swarming with holidaymakers, bungalows, chalets and caravans, in the 1930s it was a quiet holiday resort where Mim and the girls could swim and Renee could wear colourful beach pyjamas startling the conservative neighbours. Even more startling was the advent of some of Mim's dancers and Mim herself who pranced about the garden and along the beach with Bacchanalian abandon.

Over the years a whole series of early Rambert dancers came to stay at Russet Cottage as the long low building was called. There was plenty of room but the walls were very thin. Maude Lloyd on a visit recalled being given the room next to Mim. Ashley seldom appeared but on one occasion when he did come down from London she could hear him making advances to Mim who in her clear voice could be heard protesting, 'No, *no*'. The poor man was banished to a separate bungalow 'in order that he can have privacy for his writing', the visitors were told. Liz Schooling, a rich girl, thought the bungalows 'horrid'. When Antony Tudor and his lover Hugh Laing came down they were furious because they had been given separate rooms. There was a row which terminated only when another bed was moved in by the grumbling sniffy maids who had to shift the furniture around in order that the beds could be next to each other.

The respectable Dymchurch seasiders must have been intrigued by this collection of noisy adult sprites, leaping and turning, plunging in and out of the waves, striking graceful poses for the benefit of a camera or just for fun. On one occasion both Mim and Fred got stung by jelly-fish and it is not difficult to imagine the uproar this created. On warm bright nights they all cavorted around the garden and around each other like dervishes at a feast and one, more raucous than the others, shrieking with delight at the outrageous antics of Freddy Ashton doing an imitation of La Nijinska. Mim 'let off the leash' revelled in these visits. In a moment of inspiration, Fred draped her in a white tablecloth and plucking bindweed from the hedge twined it into a wreath, plonked it on her head and told her, 'Now you're Taglioni'. Dead on cue Mim took up a romantic pose and assumed the pensive, vacuous expression of a nineteenth-century Sylphide. Paul Dukes turned up occasionally and would do his Yoga exercises in the dining-room. When Mim sent the girls to ask him to have his photograph taken doing a lift with her they returned and announced, 'Uncle Paul's standing on his head again'. No doubt Rambert imperiously ordered him to attend to her and he dutifully swung her round the lawn. She clearly enjoyed hurling herself at him with her habitual cry of 'catch me' and being caught in the fish-dive which he handled with no trouble at all. The girls joined in the fun, although it is hard to imagine Renee doing anything other than sunning herself and wondering at these fascinating people into whose world she had strayed. Paul posed for the camera holding Lulu in a lift and taught both girls acrobatics on the beach. At the end of the day they all piled into the kitchen where Mim produced her delicious omelettes, her one and only culinary creation.

The children often went down alone with Renee and the maids. One evening they were sitting at the kitchen table happily playing cards when suddenly a little white face appeared at the window. Lulu cried out thinking it was a ghost and began to cry. It was Mim who on the spur of the moment had come down from London. She seemed distraught, perhaps there had been yet another upset with Ashley. She was unwelcome, and a disturbance to the peace of the little gathering round the table, which was sad.

Someone wrote that Ashley Dukes was 'the warm sunny wall against which the peach tree of Rambert's life ripened'. This may have been true in the early days of their marriage and the Mercury, but once the marriage had cooled his interest in ballet gradually ebbed away. Not that he did not remain loyal to her, but he had his own destiny to fulfil. He was not prepared to jettison his own ambitions in favour of devoting himself entirely to the furtherance of English ballet. Why should he? His interest lay in the theatre of drama and poetic drama especially. As it was she was indebted to him for his help but she would have to continue her journey largely on her own. Until he abandoned her for Sadler's Wells Fred Ashton filled the vacuum. For a time they were each other's 'sunny wall'.

CHAPTER 13

In the thirties people thought men who danced were a bit odd, even ridiculous. They admired Fred Astaire, the most graceful and balletic tap dancer ever, and liked the virility of Gene Kelly, but grown men who pranced about in tights, particularly Englishmen, well! It was all right for small boys dressed in frilly white silk shirts and velvet trousers to learn the social dances and cavort around with little girls but if later they showed the slightest sign that they might actually take dancing seriously their parents (usually the father), firmly stamped on these 'sissy' ideas. Once he had grown up such a man needed courage and determination to ignore a particularly English prejudice.

There was something about Mim that attracted men who wanted to dance. Perhaps it had to do with her time with the Russians and Poles who did not see anything unusual or strange in men dancing. She did not question their motives or indeed their sexuality, the only thing she questioned was their talent. For some of the men who came to the Mercury their best years for training had already passed them by. Those valuable years had been spent getting through school exams, studying for a different occupation, perhaps sneaking off in the evening to snatch the odd ballet class. There were very few young boys being trained at that time and the best of them graduated to Ninette de Valois.

Mim did not care for sheer athleticism, and although she appreciated a well trained dancer they had to have something more. Those young men who found their way to Notting Hill Gate discovered in her a sympathy perhaps based on her own early frustrations. Like her they had longed to be dancers and like her they did not necessarily have the perfect physical attributes. They were fired by her almost fanatical commitment and were prepared to go through the painful experience of forcing their protesting bodies to accept the discipline of daily, exacting rituals of exercise. They also had to develop a visual memory training unique to the ballet, at the same time learning, without the aid of notes, the terminology that differentiates this particular art from any other. They punished their bodies, wrenching unwilling hip-joints, pulling out tight muscles, risking injury in their effort to turn, to leap, to balance at perilous angles on one foot.

There was John Andrewes, for instance. In 1932 he was studying for a degree at Cambridge University when he met and fell in love with a beautiful girl who was studying with Rambert. He'd seen the de Basil Ballets Russes and had become an ardent balletomane. At eighteen, having decided the thing he wanted most in the world was to dance, he approached Mim who with her devastating honesty told him he was too old and advised him to stay on at Cambridge. Nevertheless, he persevered and was finally accepted for training. His family strongly objected and called in the family solicitor to talk him out of it. Much to their annoyance the solicitor simply said, 'If you want to do it, do it.' John never took his degree, and with great patience and good humour went through the arduous penance of training. I recall when as a fourteen-year-old I had graduated to the eleven o'clock professional class dear John was labouring away in the back row. When it came to the men's *tours en l'air*, a regular diversion would be the thunderous crash as John landed yet again in a heap on the floor. Being a gentleman he always apologised as he got himself back on his feet. When it came to the *tours* we all learnt to give him a wide berth in those overcrowded classes. I don't remember if he ever did master this trick but he became a very useful member of the company, and an excellent stage-manager. Nor do I know what became of his beautiful enticer but he happily married Olivia Sarel, another member of the company.

Many of the Rambert men, realising they could never achieve the standard of those who had received an early training, showed a talent for creativity way beyond the capacity of their younger, more agile brothers in ballet. They wanted more from dance than simply jumping, posturing, pirouetting and performing a series of perfect entrechats. Harold Turner, a north country boy who came to her at sixteen, was almost fully trained. He was a fine technical dancer who could clear the Mercury stage with one leap, but perhaps because she felt she could not mould him into the kind of expressive artist she needed, he did not interest her. However, she was glad enough to have him in the early days before the ethos of the Rambert style evolved. When he joined the Sadler's Wells company he felt at home being given the brio work at which he excelled.

Rambert started a tradition of training adult men which remained a particular feature of the Rambert school long after she had left the scene. Not that she was ever interested in founding traditions, 'It's an awful shortcoming in my nature', she once said in an interview, 'I cannot look into the future... it's absolutely beyond me.' Léonide Massine during the period between leaving and rejoining Diaghilev had settled in London and was teaching whilst dancing and choreographing for revues and musicals.

He had an enormous influence on promoting dance as an occupation for young men and he sent many of his most interesting pupils to Mim. He did not have much time for the English as dancers, they were one of the best audiences in the world but he considered they lacked dance temperament and facility. Their place was sitting out front not joining in. Neither did he care for Ninette de Valois whom he considered cold, a good manager but lacking the heart of a dancer, but he appreciated the work Rambert was doing. Mim had about her that astonishing aura of vitality, inspirational enthusiasm and also the power to call out dormant qualities that she perceived existed in people. When Robert Browning created the Pied Piper he must have had a vision of Marie Rambert.

And yet she could be strangely hostile to physical talent. Perhaps she was afraid of it, afraid to reveal her own shortcomings as a classical teacher? Nor could she offer a strong dancer a fitting framework in which to display his talents. Alexis Rays, a Lithuanian from South Africa, was a perfectly proportioned young classical dancer who came to her in 1935. Although endowed with beautiful feet and a natural feeling for classicism Alex irritated Mim because she thought him conceited and unintelligent. He hated her because she yelled at him in class and called him a 'dourak' (Russian for idiot). For a sixteen-year-old this was humiliating, especially as he had been a star pupil in South Africa. After a couple of terms he flounced off to Preobrajenska in Paris, then changed his name to Alexis Rassine and later joined Sadler's Wells and rose to the status of *premier danseur*, partnering Margot Fonteyn. Both he and Turner needed a company that performed the great classical ballets, Mim with her tiny Mercury stage could not accommodate them and neither of them had the ability to choreograph. On the other hand, when the handsome sixteen-year-old Frank Staff arrived from South Africa in 1933 with less technique than Rassine but more intelligence, Mim warmed to him and he stayed for several years. But he did have a talent for choreography.

Not all the Rambert men had visualised becoming dancers. Walter Gore was an early recruit who came to Mim when he was twenty. A strange, fair-haired, rather remote young man who rarely spoke, he would amuse himself between classes by playing with his model train set on the Mercury stage. He had the blank anonymous face of the actor, and indeed was descended from four generations of Scottish theatre people. His real name was Robert Taylor, but he changed it because there was a film star of that name. He lived and breathed theatre. Along with his parents, he had been part of what was then known as 'fit-up theatre' with roll-up scenery, gas lighting, and often performed on flat trucks which served as a stage. His family were poor and their little son learnt about the hard life of the touring theatre early when he was carried on stage at three months. He went to school in the day and acted at night and stayed working with his parents until he was fourteen when he was sent to the Italia Conti school to train as an actor. He didn't really want to dance but Massine, to whose classes he had gone, persuaded him and Ashton introduced him to Mim. He became a fine dancer and mime and after he left Rambert (poor Mim) in 1935 for Sadler's Wells his acting talent was well appreciated by de Valois who cast him as the Rake in her brilliant ballet *The Rake's Progress*. He returned to choreograph several more ballets for Rambert and of the English choreographers of the twentieth century who never received the recognition they deserved Walter Gore must be the foremost.

Antony Tudor came to Rambert for training in 1928. As was so often the case it was a chance visit to see the Diaghilev company that inspired him to give up his accountancy job in Smithfield market and devote the rest of his life to choreography. A Londoner, his real name was William Cook and at first Rambert was not particularly impressed with him, at twenty he was too old and although she noted his 'poetic eyes' he was not really her type of person. A clerk at a meat market was hardly a recommendation to Mim, his low-key personality did not seem to be particularly attractive and at first she was doubtful about taking him on, but he had an intensity that eventually won her over. When he told her that in spite of working in the meat market from five in the morning until mid-afternoon he was quite prepared to travel right across London for a four o'clock class she was disarmed. He had no money whatsoever so she offered him a scholarship in return for acting as secretary to the Ballet Club, and as caretaker, and on discovering he could play the piano, accompany classes whenever needed. Antony was homeless so she allowed him to live in a small room behind the stage where there was just enough room for a narrow bed. For a while he was virtually the house slave.

Agnes de Mille wrote that, 'Tudor was exploited in every way.' Well, so was everyone else if one likes to look at it in that light. Tudor may have chafed at his subservient position, but he had a goal in sight, he needed the training and if he was looked down upon because he was poor and his accent slightly 'off' he was not too bothered, perhaps it was easier for him to accept an almost monk-like existence (he was later to become a Buddhist). His material needs were few, his artistic needs limitless. This self-effacing young man, with the lean looks of the aesthete, dressed in baggy old grey trousers, worn shoes, and who bit his finger nails was a strange grey figure to whom nobody at first paid much attention. He was happy to be among artists in an atmosphere that fascinated him, although his relationship with Mim would never be as easy as Ashton's. Fred was chic and witty, Antony was heavy-going; Fred was sparkle and colour, Antony sombre without social mores although always courteous. She found him too reserved, he found her invasive, but he listened and learnt from her and worked so hard that he learnt in two years what other students took four to learn and he was already teaching classes by 1930.

When Hugh Laing came to the Mercury in 1932 it could be likened to a stick of dynamite entering a munitions factory. A sensationally handsome twenty-year-old, born in Barbados of British parents, his real name was Hugh Skinner. He had come to London to study at art school when he happened to be drawn into 'standing about and looking beautiful' in a school performance for Helen Wingrave, a teacher of historical dancing. He was so taken with the rehearsals that he decided to leave art college and become a dancer, and took his early training with Wingrave. My memory of Hugh is in the morning professional class when he provided an almost daily diversion from the daily grind. This overconfident Adonis with jet black hair, challenging black eyes and an obstinate mouth always took up the most prominent place at the barre which surrounded the evil smelling coke boiler as of divine right. It was the warmest place in the freezing studio of winter and although there was room for another person nobody dared occupy it, except Mim who would stand in front of Hugh and try to correct him. She was the fuse which ignited the fiery Barbadian and while the rest of us laboured away at our *battements tendues* we furtively watched this daily encounter from under our eyelids. All was quiet until the moment when Mim made a face and squealed, '*NO* Hugh, not like that' at Hugh's offending foot, by no means the perfect dancer's foot. 'What do you mean? *NO*? it won't go any further and there's no need to shout' Hugh hissed between his teeth.

'But what you are doing is *HORRIBLE*! I gave you the same correction yesterday and you have done *NOTHING* about it!' Mim shouts above the banging of the piano.

'I've told you I can't do any better, *GO AWAY*!' By now the voices have been raised several octaves. Mim turns purple and stands in front of him defiant. 'How dare you speak to me like that!'

Hugh picks up his towel and marches out of the studio followed by a furious Mim shouting at him all the way into the dressing-room which leads straight from the studio. Having completed the exercise we hang around sniggering and exchanging remarks while the pianist sighs deeply, rubbing her cold hands together and grabbing a furtive cigarette. The furore echoes through the door. After a while Mim reappears and demands to know why we are not practising. Hugh may or may not eventually emerge from the dressing-room but it will certainly be at his convenience and not at hers.

Temperamental outbursts are taken philosophically by the Russians but the English are less tolerant and a student, no matter his age, would be dismissed from the class, possibly expelled. This sort of behaviour, particularly in the thirties when students dared not open their mouths or even question a correction, was an affront not easily forgiven in the tight-lipped atmosphere of an English training establishment, where no allowances were made for what is loosely called the artistic temperament. Mim's reactions to Hugh's outbursts although by no means taken philosophically were perhaps better understood by her, but nonetheless humiliating in front of the other students, and she had to swallow her pride. It was her choice of words that was so wounding but she never changed, she got away with it to a certain extent because she was foreign. Besides, as far as Hugh was concerned he was valuable, she needed him. 'That *awful* woman', he would scream only just out of earshot.

Today's dancers are different, they have found their tongues and teachers have had to change their authoritarian, even arrogant manner but Mim would not have tolerated today's dancers.

Although Hugh Laing was far and away the most violent tempered of Rambert's men there were others standing long sufferingly at her interminable barre practice who resented her teaching methods, albeit voicing their indignation more gently. A young man who had prominent shoulder blades, 'wings', was constantly nagged about a defect he really could do nothing much about. She was fanatical about the back, quite rightly she said a straight back was the mainspring of elegance and deportment. When in the sixties I called to take her to the theatre in my car I tried to help her down the steep steps of her house, perceiving there was no rail. She was in her seventies by then and I feared for her safety. She shook my arm away indignantly, then perceiving that I was hurt explained as she slowly descended, 'The secret is in the back.'

She had very sharp fingers and was in the habit of prodding a student into whatever part of his or her anatomy was not properly aligned. It was one better than Maestro Cecchetti's stick but nonetheless painful. As she did her round of examining each student at the barre, Arthur toiling away and sensing she was approaching became aware of her black eyes boring through his back. Suddenly the dreaded finger stabbed him between the shoulder blades. This was too much for Arthur, this time he turned on her and in a shrill Lancashire accent cried, 'Don't *do* that! It hurts, and furthermore it's not doing your finger any good!' Rambert retreated somewhat startled but also amused.

The personal involvement and proximity of Mim was at times claustrophobic, once you became a member of that select coterie you had joined a religious sect. You were expected to live and breathe ballet to the exclusion of all else. The company at that time almost lived at the Mercury, Ashley was constantly bumping into Mim's 'bourgeois schoolgirls and boys' rushing round corners, cluttering up the entrance to the auditorium, weeping hunched up in a corner, interrupting his conversation with the secretary to report dramatically on another student's mishap. They got on his nerves particularly in the summer when they sat on the front step of his precious Mercury munching their sandwiches, snatching a bit of sun. He was constantly telling them off, sending them packing, it was a running feud and they loathed him. His grand actors and actresses, rehearsing in the theatre next door to the studio looked down on the dancers as from a great intellectual height, they were the great of the 'legit' theatre, the dancers of an altogether lower order.

Ashley's aspirations for his theatre and his wife's preoccupations with her own ambitions sat somewhat uncomfortably next to each other. That it succeeded as well as it did is a testimony to a mutual tolerance of the arts for each other.

CHAPTER 14

The children of the great and famous invariably complain about their
parents and their upbringing. In the case of Rambert's daughters there
was some justification. 'Great and famous' Ashley and Mim were not at
that time, but they were both ambitious and in the public eye. Mim was
certainly not the cosy earth-mother figure. She gave her daughters a
difficult time, particularly Angela, the eldest. She adored her Lu who
nevertheless found her mother's personality overpowering.

They loved school, the normality, even the ordinariness of the
atmosphere was like a breath of fresh air in contrast to the intellectual
hot-house of their home life. They were first sent to Notting Hill High School
which they enjoyed, but when it moved to new, modern premises in Ealing
they were removed. Ealing, besides being too far away, was considered 'too
suburban' by their parents so they were sent to Norland Place, a far more
up-market school and near to home. They were eleven and nine years old
by that time and found it difficult to make new friends since they were not
allowed to invite other children home. Mim and Ashley would not tolerate
strange children running around the place, there being no garden and no
playroom in the house.

Angela related how on one occasion they were both invited to tea by a
fellow pupil. They were taken to the Express Dairy where they ate fish and
chips for the first time in their lives. They came home bursting to tell their
parents what a wonderful time they had had. Mim and Ashley were
horrified and when the girls asked if they could invite their friend back to
tea Mim said, 'Certainly not, such common people'. When it came to this
child's birthday party she did not invite Lulu and Angela telling them flatly,
'I'm not inviting you because you've never invited me back to your house!'
It was to be like that all through their childhood, their parents' snobbery
coupled with a hearty dislike of children meant that it was a lonely
childhood excluded from many of the ordinary activities of other children.
Even in the ballet class they suffered from the burden of being 'teacher's
children' and although occasionally a dancing child might be invited back
for tea, there was a strained atmosphere generated by the singularity of
Mim and Ashley.

Neither of the girls had suitable physiques for classical ballet although Lulu had her Uncle Paul's loose limbs and back and he taught her acrobatics. Although not pretty by conventional standards she had a kind of gamine quality that was later to inspire Frank Staff to cast her as Peter in his danced version of *Peter and the Wolf*. More independent than Angela, once she grew old enough to make up her own mind, and after serving an apprenticeship with the company, she shook off the yoke of Rambertism and studied tap dancing, at which she excelled, with Buddy Bradley. Mim was very supportive and in fact it was typical of her wide interest in dance forms that she often accompanied Lu to class and watched, fascinated by yet another novel experience.

Angela was not suitable material for, nor indeed wanted to take up ballet as a profession. She was like her Aunt Renee academically clever but suffered the same fate as her aunt inasmuch as when in her teens Renee advised that Angela should be sent to university Ashley refused to consider it. He had just lost quite a large sum on an abortive enterprise taking T.S. Eliot's *Murder in the Cathedral* to New York and said he could not afford university fees; a strange repetition of his sister's own experience. So both children were coerced into becoming dancers and in Angela's case suffered a great deal of anguish in the process. Far from giving her eldest daughter any encouragement Rambert seemed to go out of her way to criticise and even humiliate Angela. Strange that, in many respects, such a warm and loving woman could be so cruel to her own daughter. Perhaps having been frustrated in her desire to be a dancer herself she wanted to force her daughters to make up for her own thwarted ambition.

Ashley distanced himself from the 'ballet lot', intent on developing his own plans for his Poetic Theatre. He took only a cursory interest in what his daughters were doing. Had Angela gone to university and Lulu become an actress it is certain that he would have taken an active part in their development. It was left to Renee to devote herself to them and run the household. When they were small the girls were almost overawed at Mim's smartness. Angela recalled that 'she came to say goodnight before going to the theatre in a most spectacular pink satin dress with the then fashionable dropped waist and a large bunch of pink artificial flowers on one hip. Her sleek black hair was cut in an Eton crop and her mouth painted in the shape of a bright red rosebud. We were not allowed to kiss her on the mouth but in Polish fashion on both cheeks.' This was in the early days of the marriage when Mim and Ashley regularly attended first nights and led an active social life, typical of that milieu. The children were never neglected as there were maids in the house and their aunt Renee, but one wonders whether Mim ever took them to buy an ice-cream or for a walk in the park. She was to do all of this in later life for her grandchildren whom she adored but it was left to distant and strange Renee to take Angela and Lulu to school, to oversee their homework, to take them down to Dymchurch for the holidays. Renee loved her two little nieces but was inhibited about being demonstrative and disliked all forms of physical contact. The girls did not share their confidences, their worries or the confusions of puberty with their maiden aunt, and their parents were busy and must not be bored with such things. The girls were very close at this period and Lulu adored her big sister. Later when Mim's preference for Lulu became more and more evident there was to be a schism between the sisters which Lulu resolved by quitting England with her husband and children and spending the rest of her life first in Trinidad where she ran a ballet school, and later in Spain, eventually, after Rambert's death, settling with her husband in Tenerife.

I was about eleven years old when my mother and I watched a Sunday night performance of the Ballet Club in 1932. With four years of Cecchetti training behind me my mother had considered sending me to Ninette de Valois, however she changed her mind when the mother of a pupil at that school warned that de Valois tended to cow her pupils. 'I'm not going to let anyone cow Brigitte!' my mother said firmly. She'd heard of Madame Rambert and on enquiry she was informed that although Madame was fiery of temperament she did not attempt to stifle the individuality of her pupils, in fact she liked a bit of spirit, and so I was enrolled for the children's afternoon class.

I have no memory of being auditioned. Rambert would not accept an ill-proportioned or unattractive child and we had all received some previous training. These classes included those she hoped were the material for her next generation of Rambert dancers. If a child was not accepted it was quite often simply on the grounds of their appearance. Mim incurred the everlasting hatred of a mother whose infant prodigy was turned down. 'Oh well, yes, she has been well trained', Mim said to her secretary who had the unlucky task of dealing with the mother. 'But those dreadful protruding teeth! Like a horse!' She was right in that with her Sunday night audiences sitting so close to the stage in that small auditorium her dancers had to be good-looking and she was single minded in her pre-occupation with her company. Another talented little girl with big blue eyes and her blonde hair in ringlets was also rejected because Mim thought her precocious. 'And you know ... those black eyelashes ... with blonde hair! She was made-up, and that *awful* pushy mother!'

An older girl came to watch a morning class with her mother. She remembered how appalled they were at the sight of 'This little old woman dressed in a tatty pink tutu, baggy pink tights and wearing dirty old pointe shoes on her hideous big feet!' The get-up that Rambert wore to teach her professional class in those days must have been an effort to look 'classical.' It was an aberration for someone with such impeccable taste. The origins of the tutu probably belonged to some long-forgotten production and, always thrifty in her habits, she saw no reason to buy new ballet shoes when so many, and to her perfectly adequate, pointe shoes hung discarded in the dressing-room. She was about forty at the time but after the girl's pretty young teacher in Leamington Spa this was a shock.

When the class terminated Mim interviewed the girl and after scrutinising her face said, 'If you want to teach I will take you but if you want to dance – go away.' When the girl said indignantly that she did want to dance Mim almost pushed her and her mother out of the studio. There was no question that Mim could be abominably rude and it is not surprising that this dancer, who did in spite of this have a career as Barbara Vernon, loathed Mim for evermore. It was perhaps a bit unfortunate that she later married a dancer, John Gregory, who did not have a good word to say about Rambert.

As an eleven-year-old newcomer I was overawed by the studio more than by the class itself. I stared up at a vaulted roof, supported by large dark oak beams that straddled across the area under which we danced, the light came from a big Gothic window high up at one end of the studio below which hung a long, faded, woven tapestry depicting an idyllic hunting scene. Below stood a Florentine robing chest on which Madame sat teaching. Behind the chest hung the only mirror in the room, a large gilded drawing-room mirror, the silvered glass speckled with black patches of age.

For the children's class we faced the other way so that parents could watch. There was another window on the side wall and the ecclesiastical atmosphere engendered by the Gothic architecture of the windows and doors, the diffused quality of the light that filtered in, the echo created by the height of what was really a hall, induced a feeling of reverence which no doubt impressed the parents with an appropriate respect for the art of dance. Along the wall on the other side of the studio there were three identical heavy Gothic-style doors. Behind the first door was the vault-like dressing-room in which we changed, the second door led into a cupboard. Legend has it that during a particularly acrimonious exchange between Rambert and Hugh, Mim in a fit of rage threw herself into the cupboard instead of into Hugh's small dressing-room. This was behind the third door which had originally been the priest's robing room when the hall was used as the Sacristy to the church.

Dominating the scene was a big furnace squatting on its own concrete dais surrounded by the metal railing which doubled as a barre. The furnace was in fact the star performer since it heated the entire building and had to be stoked up at regular and often inconvenient moments. The 'donkey' was given to unpredictable moods and smells and like a malevolent aunt glowered at the humans hopping around it. It was a monstrous contradiction to the austere elegance of the rest of the studio. The people who accompanied the children sat on one side of the donkey on tip-up theatre seats under a huge painting of the infant Moses in the bullrushes. On the other side stood the second-hand upright piano pushed up close to the fire in winter in the vain hope that it would warm the frozen pianist.

Mim was at her most delightful in those afternoon classes when she wore a more suitable blouse and skirt and heeled shoes. We children were her hope and joy, slightly unsteady colts eager to please, and we were praised in open admiration if we did well. Of course she herself, Madame show-off, was delighted to have an audience. She taught us some of the dances from the classics, the Chinese Dance from *Aurora* where we bobbed up and down idiotically nodding our heads in time to the rhythm and pretending to fan ourselves. We charged across the floor in the cygnet foursome from *Swan Lake*, a nightmare of precision dancing which challenged our fragile pointe-work and which we viewed with some scepticism. The other three cygnets in my group were Lulu, Deborah Dering and Sally Gilmour. Deborah and Sally had been passed on to Rambert by Karsavina when she gave up teaching. Deborah was considered the more promising of the two, half Russian, a tall slim child with long arms and legs, the face of a Madonna and a lovely classical line. Rambert had high hopes of producing a ballerina. No one paid much attention to little Sally who though well proportioned was not really a classical type and did not have strong feet. Unobtrusive, she had the wide eyes and toothiness of a small animal and indeed it was she who was to make a name for herself as Mrs Tebrick in Howard's *Lady into Fox*. Deborah, whose heart was not really in ballet, gave up quite young to marry Robin Guthrie, the painter.

We all took part in the earliest television programme of ballet transmitted from Alexandra Palace in 1936 when I danced the Sugar Plum Fairy variation, one of several solos and extracts from some of the Ballet Club repertoire. When Colonel de Basil's Ballets Russes started to perform at Covent Garden Opera House Rambert would take a few chosen pupils to matinees. Rambert never worried about 'fairness', as far as talent was concerned there was no such thing, talent must be nurtured and inspired, it was the passport to favour and the favoured ones were Sally, Deborah, Angela and Lulu, myself and two or three others. We sat at the side near the stage in the stalls circle and for me it was the most thrilling experience of my life. The ballerinas were Alexandra Danilova, Irina Baronova, Tamara Toumanova and Tatiana Riabouchinska and they had created a sensation. The last three 'baby ballerinas', not much older than ourselves, danced with astonishing virtuosity. And the men! My attitude towards male dancers had not been particularly complimentary, but when I watched Massine, Lichine, Shabelevsky and a host of other virile male dancers I revised my opinion. The proximity of our seats to the stage made it possible to examine not only the dancers at close quarters but also their make-up , which was much heavier than is the fashion now. The eyes of the women shaded with thick false eyelashes looked enormous, and they reshaped the contours of their faces, even their noses, with cleverly applied shadow and highlighting. They looked exotic, mysterious, super-humans belonging to a world of fantasy.

The combination of wonderful music, the settings, and above all the liveliest, most dramatic merging of dance, character and mime, enchanted and excited me to the point that I emerged from these performances in a dream-like trance, unable to speak. It made me understand Rambert's passion for Russian ballet, her courage in trying to recreate this magic in her dancers, and the sometimes agonising frustration she suffered in trying to get her phlegmatic, materially complacent pupils to show even a spark of temperament in their dancing. If they did, it all came from her. For my part I resolved that one day I would join the Ballets Russes.

CHAPTER 15

During the years of my training my mother and I saw many performances by ballet companies, the Sadler's Wells company which we attended regularly, the Ballet Jooss, a great favourite and later the Markova-Dolin company, but it is those Sunday evening Ballet Club performances which occupy a special place in my memory, perhaps because at eleven it was my first experience and like a first love that memory lingers. The intimacy of the atmosphere in the small auditorium reminded me of the little cardboard theatre I cherished at home, where I delighted in moving colourful cut-out figures across the stage, changing the wings, dropping down the red painted curtain, inventing my own stories. I recall those gem-like ballets as magical scenes enclosed in the confines of a crystal paperweight.

Some of the ballets still come to mind easier than others. The first one surely must have been Antony Tudor's *Lysistrata* in 1932. I have a fleeting vision of Pearl Argyle, the beautiful Pearl, sitting in a Grecian frieze pose on a seat in front of the backcloth, a vague memory of Tudor himself bearded and handsome in a clever make-up. Antony always looked good on stage, never attempting difficult technical dancing but projecting interesting images of some dignity. Diana Gould, militant, aggressive and vaguely unpleasant, seemed too large for that limited space, handsome though she was. Billy Chappell's designs for this ballet were colourful, reminding me of the designs on the Greek vases I had pictures of at home in my *Myths and Legends of Ancient Greece*. I was a little shocked at the absence of the ballet dresses I was familiar with, and the movements to my young eyes, schooled to the classical technique, seemed jerky, staccato, almost uncoordinated, and Prokofiev's music was quite beyond me. I wasn't sure if I liked *Lysistrata* but I was awakened to the diversities of ballet.

I was less disturbed by Ashton's *A Florentine Picture*. Here they were, those barefoot dancers of Rambert's early days, eight beautiful girls drifting from one carefully sculpted group to form another. And in their midst Mim, again as the Virgin Mary. The designs were traditional pastel-tinted diaphanous tunics, lit in a golden light, a perfect evocation of Botticelli's paintings. They moved gently to the music of Corelli. The ballet was nicknamed 'Flossie' by the dancers. The simplicity of the vocabulary did not overtax them but required a style that would later always single out Ashton's understanding of pure flowing movement and demonstrated Isadora's influence on his work.

Andrée Howard's ballet *Mermaid* in collaboration with Susan Salaman, based on the story of Hans Andersen's *Little Mermaid,* was enchanting. Andrée was exceptionally musical and the choice of Ravel's *Introduction and Allegro* for the underwater scenes and the shipwreck followed by his *Alborada del Gracioso* for the palace scene was an extraordinary matching, the music could have been written for the ballet. I can still picture Pearl as the mermaid, her head encased in a gauzy helmet which emphasised her perfect bone structure. A grey tight-fitting dress whose skirt formed a tail was made of crinkly, clinging cotton that had to be dampened and rolled every night after the performance to ensure that it did not stretch and would cling to her legs – legs as beautiful as Danilova's famous legs. Andrée's designs and skilful lighting gave an impression of the eerie light deep down in the ocean. Behind a dimly lit gauze the mermaid seemed to swim across our view, frolicking with her sister mermaids . The gauze lifted to reveal a ship tossed in a turbulent sea – or so it seemed so clever was Andrée's choreography. The ship was no more than a long plank on which was mounted a tall mast with a sail attached, almost Eastern in its economy. A critic wrote, 'with the total absence of stage machinery, the scene of the shipwreck was rendered with extraordinary forcefulness'. Billy Chappell as the Prince manipulated the sail in such a way as to indicate a violent storm, thrashing to and fro, rolling from side to side, a masterpiece of invention, simplicity itself. Finally he keeled over and disappeared in the darkening storm, drifting, drowning while the gauze gently dropped down again to reveal the Prince floating inanimate supported by the mermaids. The illusion of water behind the gauze was astonishing for such a small, close theatre and achieved thanks to Ashley Dukes's care in installing the best lighting-board money could buy. The next scene was set on the terrace of the Palace conveyed simply by a painted wing, a white balustrade against a cobalt blue backdrop, sufficient to give an impression of sunshine, luxury and space.The Prince and his fiancée (Schooling) led a formal Spanish style dance with his courtiers dressed in deep reds and blacks and the women wearing mantillas.

Suddenly they were arrested mid-step when a diaphanous chiffon scarf like a small wave was tossed in the air behind the balustrade. The dance continued, then again the same occurrence stopped them in their tracks, this time the mermaid appeared as though rising from the sea. Pearl must have lain behind that balustrade for some time before she finally appeared, stiff and cold as only a dancer can be, forced to stay in a cramped and uncomfortable position waiting for their entrance, but for me, a wide eyed child who loved her fairy stories, this was magic, the thought never crossed my mind – neither did it cross the minds of the spellbound audience, such is the illusion of theatre.

The mermaid, now bereft of her tail, tottered across the stage on pointe wincing at each step, her hand held against her cheek. We all felt the pain of this faltering walk. 'At each step you will feel as though walking on daggers', she had been warned. Ashton borrowed this walk for Margot Fonteyn in *Ondine*, and many other moments, his production plainly inspired by Andrée's *Mermaid*.

Although many of these early ballets adapted quite well when later they were presented on larger stages, *Mermaid* was not among them. This was an intimate ballet, perfection in its own way, a ballet with which the audience closely involved itself, but something of the magic, the poignancy of the story was lost on the way.

When at the 75th anniversary I met Olivia Sarel, now both of us quite elderly ladies, we peered at each other in the darkened auditorium and smiled in recognition. When Olivia said, 'Do you remember *Rape?* That awful table?' We collapsed into giggles like two schoolgirls. Andrée created her witty ballet *The Rape of the Lock* just at the time when as a fourteen-year- old I had graduated to becoming a member of the company. Based on a poem by Alexander Pope, the music was Haydn's *Clock Symphony*. I had the misfortune to be cast as one of four sylphs, misfortune because I was taller than the other three who were of the average Rambert size, just over five foot. I had the misfortune of being 5' 4" and was still growing. Andrée was irritated by this and ordered me to *bourée* on bent knees to keep the same height as the others, luckily the pink net skirts were calf length. Andrée was difficult to work for during rehearsals, her instructions tended to be vague and she got annoyed if we didn't immediately understand what she had in mind. Little more than a raw student, I was lost and awkward and she nagged me incessantly. Our main function was to teeter around on pointe getting in everyone's way. The card game was the highlight of the ballet when Belinda (Pearl Argyle) beat the Baron, (Tudor) splendidly attired as were the others in eighteenth-century costume. Andrée had the brilliant idea of turning us sylphs into table legs by crouching uncomfortably under a square baize-covered table-top. We had to stay in this position with our chins tucked into our chests, curled up with the table resting on the back of our heads. Being bigger than the others I could not get onto their level and therefore the board was constantly tilting while the principals were having their game of cards. It was uncomfortable for the others but for me it was torture. I daresay it was quite a clever ballet but it did not stay for long in the repertory. Another one of Andrée's less successful ballets was *La Muse s'amuse* in which we ladies at a tea party wore black Edwardian dresses and large black pancake hats which kept falling off whenever we moved. I have to confess that I dreaded working for Andrée.

It was the fashion in the thirties to insert a series of divertissements not just to fill out the programme but also to give an opportunity for individual dancers to be seen by the audience. Andrée danced a delightful solo arranged for her by Ashton called *Pompette*. The costume, designed by Andrée herself, was black and pink, elbow length black gloves, saucy black hat with a pink ostrich feather tilted at a rakish angle over one eye. Holding a liqueur glass and provokingly kicking up her silk-stockinged legs the dancer revolved around a delicate gilt chair. It was Ashton in his smart twenties mood – no one ever did it better, the humour, the chicness and the sheer fun of it very much in the style of *Façade* which he had produced the previous year in 1931.

Foyer de danse was sheer delight. Ashton's recreation of the Degas paintings, the dancers (later including myself), adored appearing in it. They could literally let their hair down. Suzette Morfield in particular let hers tumble down to her waist and could have been Degas's model. Dressed in flattering three-quarter-length white net dresses with bright, wide satin sashes, each girl a different colour, big bows like bustles on their *derrières* and with a black velvet ribbon round their throat, they looked perfect Paris Opéra coryphées. It was the kind of ballet that every little girl had imagined for herself when she started her training. Each dancer was encouraged to look their prettiest, all frou-frou and bows. Here you saw the logic of Mim's single-mindedness in picking pretty dancers. Alicia Markova played the ballerina and Fred himself relished the role of the mannered, fussy nineteenth-century ballet master, baton in hand, demonstrating some very acceptable entrechats.

Ashton's *Mephisto Valse* to Liszt's music of that name was an unusual ballet, the dramatic tension set by the pounding of feet, like the pounding of horse's hooves behind the curtains before they opened onto a darkened room inside a cottage. Sophie Fedorovitch perfectly matched Liszt's dark, brooding score working to a limited palette of black, white, grey and terracotta. Figures moved in the dim light whispering, observing, clustering round a delicate, frail girl. Dressed in white tulle, her huge dark eyes gazing shyly from under a little white veil, her black hair smoothed against her small head wreathed in large white marguerites, Markova was beautiful and touching in a role created for her by Ashton. Walter Gore played her handsome, sympathetic Faust while Fred only just got away with his role of the devil. He did his best to look evil in a little black hat and a short cloak over white tights which by today's standards would be considered rather camp. Nonetheless this was a dramatic and quite sinister work not perhaps characteristic of his later ballets.

Ninette de Valois's *Bar aux Folies-Bergère* produced in 1934, was fun, unashamed entertainment revealing the 'show-biz' side of de Valois's apprenticeship in the commercial theatre which probably never surfaced again in her subsequent choreography. The most striking moment was when the curtains parted to reveal a perfect reproduction of Manet's famous painting. Pearl Argyle was the girl behind the bar, lovely in a blonde wig. When she left to go to the Wells the role was taken over by Elisabeth Schooling who so resembled the painting that she might have been Manet's model. Markova danced the lead role of La Goulue, the raucous red-haired leader of the can-can so vividly portrayed by Toulouse-Lautrec. It was a strange bit of casting, anybody less like the character could not have been found. Markova, in a black-and-mauve froth of net and wearing a very smart Ascot style black hat, tripped saucily round the stage on her pointes looking more like the sales manageress in a house of *haute couture*! No matter, the audience thoroughly enjoyed themselves, Markova revealed an unexpected sense of humour brought out by Ashton playing the outrageous waiter.

The thing was that ballet as entertainment was never out of context, Mim understood that if you intend to interest audiences in new, and in the case of Tudor, intense 'message' choreography, you also have to understand the importance of allowing the audience to relax and enjoy themselves. Humour in ballet is scarce and the Ballet Club repertoire at that time was unique in that it included sophisticated wit and dancers who could put it across. *Façade* was an instance of this, Ashton's humour was at its highest and each number produced chuckles from the audience that I never heard again once it was moved to bigger theatres, and a different company.

Before every performance Mim would rush round to the dressing-room in order to check on her dancers' make-up and appearance – sometimes with devastating results. When at fourteen I began to perform on the Mercury stage I had no idea how to apply greasepaint and would spend ages smearing my face with too much grease and Leichner no. 5 – a deathly pale colour which I desperately tried to tone down with powder which turned into a kind of suet pudding. I circled my eyes with heavy black lines like an elderly Theda Bara and incurred Mim's despairing criticisms.

'Your face looks too big, put some shadow on your jaw.' No one told me how to do it so I gave myself a grey beard around my lower face.

'Your nose is too long darling, put some shadow under it', she complained so I added a kind of moustache.

'Your eyes are too small, put some more shadow and soap out your eyebrows and paint them on higher.'

The thing was, that apart from bits of information hurled at me from the other girls there was no one to help. Mim knew what she wanted but didn't seem to know how to get it. She had observed and admired the clever make-up of the de Basil company, 'You know she is a very plain girl but looks beautiful on stage!' she enthused about one of the Russian ballerinas. With me it was the opposite. A make-up designed for huge theatres and powerful lighting was unsuitable for that intimate little theatre. My mother was alarmed, what had happened to her pretty daughter? 'You look so ugly from the front', she complained, she could also be unsparing in her criticism. She rushed out and bought me a little make-up book from Leichner. I had a great time experimenting at home, making myself up as a Chinaman, an Arab, but a pretty girl defeated me. Today's dancer receives lessons in make-up, is even made-up by a helper but no such help was on offer in 1935. At fourteen I was expected to emerge from my scruffy teenage chrysalis into a ravishing butterfly. But no one showed me how.

We all endured the howling cries of Mim's devastating criticism. Beryl Kay, a contemporary of mine, had a very rough time from Rambert on account of a generous, and by today's standards, a sexy bosom. Mim couldn't stand this and instructed Beryl to bind her breasts down with wide bandages of cotton. 'The result was that I was one solid mass right down to my waist – like Queen Mary.' Angela, also full-busted, was told she looked like a nursing mother. Nonplussed by the look on her daughter's face she hastily added, 'but of course men like it.' The awful hemp wigs for *L'Après-midi d'un faune* were for smaller heads than mine, I appeared at the dress rehearsal wearing it as a sort of bonnet showing my black hair-line, I simply could not get it on any farther. I was instructed to bind my hair with a wide piece of white material, soap it and take my foundation right up to the edge of the wig. I was back to looking like the egghead. My mother had to endure Arnold Haskell muttering, 'What a pity – such a pretty girl.'

It was not until I joined the Ballets Russes that I finally achieved a flattering make-up, but then I had the help of my more experienced colleagues. The Russians were so much more generous with their advice. Mim was generous – too generous, but her dancers were of a meaner disposition, too busy to help a bewildered novice.

CHAPTER 16

In her memoir Rambert wrote, 'Our dancers... proved very useful to Sadler's Wells and I lost them one by one.' There is a certain irony in her use of the word 'useful' but she could write in 1982 without rancour, by then having received recognition for her work and been accorded her proper place in the history of English ballet. 'Although I had only about twenty professional pupils at that time', she continues, 'we managed to provide the Wells with Ashton, for whom as a choreographer the move represented a natural development; Pearl Argyle, Walter Gore, Harold Turner and Leslie Edwards.' Billy Chappell was in due course to follow. She must have felt desperate at times – these were not run-of-the mill dancers, they were her 'special' people chosen for their intelligence, for their understanding of the work she was doing. 'It was all very good for them', she wrote magnanimously, 'and thank heaven, we managed to replace them.' And indeed there was a constant influx of talented people who wanted to join up.

Not all the Rambert dancers found it easy to fit into other companies, their very individual qualities made them difficult to assimilate into companies with a traditional repertory of the classics. They tended to be cliquish and snobbish and a sound technique was more important than expressive qualities in the rough and tumble of a large professional company. Throughout the thirties and particularly the forties many of Mim's people stayed with her under the shelter of an environment that understood them and where their particular talents were nurtured.

Nevertheless, several of Mim's dancers were accepted by George Balanchine's Les Ballets 1933 and Betty Cuff and Elizabeth Ruxton joined the Ballets Russes de Monte-Carlo. But when later Diana Gould and Prudence Hyman joined the same company, they were most unhappy, the Russian dancers were hostile and apparently made their life difficult. To them Diana was a spoilt rich girl and they probably tarred Pru with the same brush. Both girls left after one year. When Diana heard that I had been accepted by this same company in 1937 she rang my mother begging her not to let me go as the Russians were so nasty to English dancers. Fortunately my mother took no notice. I adored working with the Russians and had the experience of my dancing life.

It has been said that Mim's dancers left her because they couldn't stand her bullying. Although this may have been true with some, most appreciated how much she helped them, admired her passionate commitment and regarded her explosive outbursts with amused tolerance. They understood her frustrations in trying to build a company without being able to provide regular employment and a regular salary. In those struggles of the early thirties she suffered agonies of hurt and frustration each time someone left the ranks and everyone, including her long-suffering husband and children, were witnesses to terrible outbursts of rage which exhausted her and everyone around her.

In 1936 Lilian Baylis wrote to Rambert who had complained furiously to her that the Wells advertised themselves as 'the only school of ballet in England attached to a theatre'. The tone of Baylis's response suggests that Rambert's letter pulled no punches. 'We're not really as bad as you imply!' she wrote. 'You didn't finish the quotation which should read, "The only school of ballet attached to a theatre *engaging a permanent company of dancers*".' She continues, 'It is the words underlined which make our claim unique, and which are an incentive to joining the school. There isn't another in the country that can offer its students the chance of working up to a living wage, and we do feel we must stress this.' Baylis continues on a placatory note, 'We know the valuable work you do – our company bears ample witness to this – but the fact that we can now offer our people a weekly wage (which is as impossible for you as it was for us before the Wells opened), does put us in a different position, and this is the distinction we wish to stress in the advertisement.'

The Ballet Club would not have been possible without most of the dancers having some kind of financial support, either from their families or from their own pockets, but they worked for no pay in the hope, even the assumption, that eventually a fully-fledged professional ballet company would be founded. But Mim and Ashley were not forthcoming on this point. They did not have the money to invest themselves and refused any offers of help fearing interference. As far as the dancers were concerned it was considered that the honour and glory of being participants should be enough. The dancers, however, thought differently and Rambert herself for many years would suffer from being dubbed 'amateur' (a word she hated) for that very reason. Agnes de Mille in her book *Dance to the Piper* observed that, 'Somehow she mismanaged matters. She had not the iron trap-like intention to force success.' This and many other shrewd but rather brutal observations incensed Rambert who took a very long time to forgive her.

The loss of her 'Darling Fred' hurt her particularly, he was an important element in her own artistic development and it is doubtful if he was ever as close to the cooler de Valois. For a while he returned to perform and rehearse his ballets but with the demands of his new employment it became increasingly difficult for him to participate fully and certainly he had no time to choreograph. His place was quickly filled by Tudor but there was never the same close relationship there.

Peggy van Praagh joined the Ballet Club in her early twenties. Her teacher had been Margaret Craske and she was one of a small number of dancers who had passed the advanced Cecchetti examination with honours – a rare distinction. She had auditioned for de Valois who had turned her down, Rambert who sat at the Cecchetti examinations had seen her work but also turned her down. Rambert respected Craske's teaching, she was the Maestro's favourite pupil and the syllabus work at the Mercury was firmly Cecchetti based and a succession of teachers of the method were hired. She would certainly have welcomed van Praagh in that capacity since in her early twenties she was already an experienced teacher, but Peggy wanted to perform. Rambert had her reservations. Although good-looking Peggy was stocky of build and although a powerful dancer had what Mim called 'heavy legs.' Furthermore Rambert was somewhat prejudiced against academic dancers whom she felt would not easily adapt to her freer concept of dance. Peggy must have been devastated at this rejection and would later bear no love for Rambert. Still, Mim sent her to Tudor when he was choreographing *Adam and Eve* for the Camargo Society. Tudor perceived in Peggy qualities that he needed for his own choreography and she became one of his core artists when he later founded his own company. Peggy eventually joined the Ballet Club but despite her brilliant technique was not allowed to dance in short skirts.

In 1941 van Praagh joined the Sadler's Wells company as dancer and teacher but she encountered the same reservations about herself from de Valois who after giving her the leading role in *Coppélia* where she could display her technique and sense of humour, gave her no more major roles. Despite this she went on to found the Australian Ballet and was to become a Dame in recognition of her services to Australian Ballet. One can imagine that Mim frowned and bit her lip on reading of this in her newspaper, but always generous of spirit she would have written a letter congratulating Peggy on her success.

Tudor had already made several ballets by the time Ashton left. *The Planets* in 1934 to Gustav Holst's music had established him as an unusual choreographic talent.

He used three of the seven pieces, *Venus, Mars* and *Neptune*, which were arranged for two pianos for which Angus Morrison was called in to second Charles Lynch. The first scene was calmly beautiful with Pearl and Billy as the loving mortals born under the planet Venus. The next scene, Mars, to the repetitive pounding march theme was startling and the intensity of Hugh Laing's performance as the mortal born under Mars was quite alarming particularly at such close quarters. Stripped to the waist, his muscular torso, his black hair swept back from a high forehead and his burning black eyes, he must have given the dowagers in the front rows quite a frisson. He leapt, twisted and twitched to the throbbing music as though possessed of a demon. Hugh Stevenson's designs for the six dancers accompanying him were stark, unattractive dresses, their hair constrained inside black skull-caps. Antony had avoided all sense of glamour and picked six of the plainest girls, grim-faced, fierce, they writhed and rolled on the floor, clenching their fists and performing angular movements that pre-empted the work of Martha Graham. The decor, costumes and lighting were predominantly red. Van Praagh was surprisingly effective as the planet, all that excess muscle that Rambert complained about was recognised by Antony as symbolising strength and power. The polite audience trembled at this display of red-hot anger.

The coolness of Neptune came as a relief, Tudor knew his theatre. This was an extraordinarily atmospheric piece of choreography in which Kyra Nijinsky as guest artist created the role of the mortal born under the planet. There were only three other dancers, Antony himself was the planet flanked on either side by two tall dancers, Rose Paget and Tamara Svetlova. He had devised an unusual passage spanning the width of the stage when all three walked in profile, *Faune* style on parallel feet with arms outstretched which they contracted and expanded slowly as they walked. Although the classical technique was Tudor's fundamental grammar, like all late starters he had learnt it in a hurry and perhaps for that very reason did not feel shackled to it. He was able to invent original movement quite unrelated to dance but often based on observation of nature and of body language. In the case of this passage in Neptune the movement had originated in his observation of the movement of the sea on his visit to Dymchurch in the early days of his relationship with Rambert. Enrolling Angela and Lulu to his cause one day on the beach he worked out the movement of the ebb and flow of the sea on them, a unique experience they never forgot.

Rambert raved over his next ballet, *The Descent of Hebe* to Ernest Bloch's First *Concerto Grosso*, which was very much her kind of music. She considered his choreography 'ravishing' and in characteristic manner would clasp her hands and close her eyes in ecstasy when describing this ballet to friends. However, his next ballet, *Jardin aux lilas* the following year, evoked a very different response. Rambert could not cope with Tudor. She who had recognised Nijinsky's choreographic genius could not see that under her nose another genius was breaking new ground. This secretive man did not confide in her and did not seek her advice although she always expected to be consulted where all her protégés' work was concerned. Antony, having by now formed a close alliance with Hugh, discussed his ideas and problems with him, and Hugh would always be his best critic for the rest of his working life. He stood sentinel, a snarling guardian, barring her intrusion to the work in progress.

She was doubtful about Tudor's choice of theme for *Jardin* which perhaps she felt was too sentimental and for the same reason she thought his choice of music, Chausson's *Poème* harkened back to the romantic age while the Ballet Club stood for the avant garde. Hugh Stevenson's décor of a collection of lilac bushes she thought obvious and commonplace, nor did she agree to the casting of van Praagh as the 'other woman' and as for Antony insisting on spraying the auditorium with cheap scent ' to give atmosphere', well, this was downright vulgar in her opinion. She need not have worried about the length of Peggy's skirt, the ballet was set in the Edwardian age. Hugh Stevenson's dresses for the women were long and formal, which was unusual for those days.

This was new territory for her and she felt insecure. Perhaps the memory of the debacle at the Champs-Élysées, the ridicule of that audience for *Sacre* raised a fear of failure in her, not that her polite upper-class English audience would in any way have behaved as discourteously as the Parisians. She was almost apologetic to them on the first night. As she said herself, she was a coward and in fearing failure for *Jardin* she failed herself. *Jardin aux lilas* was immediately hailed as a masterpiece. She would always be unsure of her own judgement, not because she did not have faith in her own perception, but because she was humble enough to recognise that she might have made a mistake.

But the tensions between Tudor and Mim did not abate. Perhaps if Hugh had not stood between her and Antony, she who understood artists so well would have come to a compromise with him. In fact he did not need her, and that was what hurt, she needed to be needed.

Agnes de Mille turned up in the eleven o'clock class one morning in 1935. A curious looking, rather ugly woman, with a hook nose, an hour-glass figure and tiny feet, she gave a quite hostile, defensive impression.

She was a strange anomaly, a sparrow amongst the canaries, whatever was Rambert thinking of taking on board this dancer who by then was well into her thirties?

My mother was by now enslaved to Madame and her dancers and had begun to help out in the cavernous little cellar in the basement which was the wardrobe for the Ballet Club. As with anyone who came into contact with Mim she found herself, with Rambert's encouragement, that diviner of talent, making many of the costumes and generally becoming more and more involved. De Mille planned to give a series of recitals in London starting at the Mercury and enlisted her to make her costumes for the recital. These turned out to be quite elaborate and de Mille was exacting in her demands, each detail, each piece of ribbon or jewellery, had to be correct. My mother allowed her to rummage around her collection of trimmings and ornaments freely and for very little money. My mother, the gentlest woman in the world, found this tough, egotistical American woman tiring, and she wasn't at all sure how good she was, neither was Rambert. Furthermore she had a 'Momma' who was equally tiresome, interfering and dictatorial.

This was an independent venture and everyone waited with curiosity to see what de Mille would produce. Hugh partnered her in a couple of the dances, there were sixteen numbers in all and Agnes carried the evening almost single-handed. She had to make frenetic quick changes and my mother was bulldozed into acting as Agnes's dresser since having made the costumes she knew how they worked. She agreed somewhat reluctantly.

When it came to the dress rehearsal she was amazed to discover that de Mille was an extraordinary and fascinating performer. 'You wouldn't believe how she transforms herself, at times she looks quite beautiful', she told me, 'She's so clever – and very funny in some of the numbers.' She could change herself from an outrageous Kurdish dancing prostitute into a sophisticated, elegant Boucher painting and back again into a Degas dancer. This last was particularly amusing as she managed to look like Degas's famous sculpture and captured the feeling perfectly. She had a chameleon-like quality that was quite unique. The setting consisted of a barre, a ladder and by means of a square of light shining from the wings, the impression of a window. On a dimly lit stage she entered walking with that peculiar duck-like walk of a dancer with aching feet and having slowly watered a small section of the floor with a minute watering can went and sat on the bottom rung of the ladder, feet turned out, her long crinkly red hair cascading down to her waist. There was no musical accompaniment, it was very private, the audience held their breath as though not wanting to be caught peeping. She wore the typical Degas white net skirt, her generous bust firmly corseted into the boned bodice, her unusually small feet emerging from the calf-length skirt. She sat rubbing her ankles while looking towards the window, by this simple pose she portrayed the temptations of the dancer fighting to keep up the discipline of training. Finally she got up and started solemnly to do her *pliés* at the wooden barre, interrupting her work from time to time to waddle over to the window. Her timing was perfect, she kept us sitting on the edge of our seats. Busily she worked through the routine of barre practice punctuated by frequent visits to the rosin box in which she rummaged around like a cat in a litter box. There were moments when she resisted going to the window and resolutely turned round and performed some frantic *petits battements* –that ridiculous, frenetic beating of the toe against the ankle of the supporting foot, then more trips to the window where she stood observing the 'activities outside'. We longed to know what was going on ourselves! After again watering the surface of the stage her attempts at perfecting pirouettes was particularly delightful. The whole study was performed in the dead-pan manner that only de Mille could perfect. I watched all the performances with fascination, each dance was carefully thought out, embracing a broad spectrum of European and American culture. I had never seen dance used in this manner, neither, I think had the audience.

Agnes became a great friend of Hugh and Antony and plainly she had quite an influence on Antony's choreography. He was increasingly becoming a cult figure to certain of the dancers and they formed a separate clique which was not altogether healthy. The men, though admirers of Tudor's work, were not necessarily followers, Frank Staff remarked that 'going to Antony's rehearsals was like going to Vespers'. He now embarked on his greatest work *Dark Elegies*, inspired by Mahler's *Kindertotenlieder* (Songs on the death of children). Rambert did not at first agree to the theme of such a ballet but Tudor was determined. She writes, 'I asked him to show me one finished song and realised how profound the choreography was.' She makes much of the ballet in her book, *Quicksilver*, going into some detail, and later would always treasure it as the greatest achievement of those early days. A deep and emotional work, this ballet was always cast from the senior dancers of the company.

The rehearsals took place in the basement studio right next to the wardrobe where the peace was frequently shattered by the appalling rows that used to take place between Hugh and Antony and also between Mim and the two of them who would shut her out of the studio. Tudor may have been a genius but apart from his adoring coterie he was not particularly liked and seemed to attract the malcontents of the school. A good teacher, he was nevertheless a bully and could be intentionally cruel, more so than Rambert who did not mean to be. He did not like women, particularly pretty women, although his close friendship with Maude Lloyd was the exception. He was agonisingly slow when working out his choreography and his cast had to be very patient. Maude wrote of *Jardin*, 'Nothing was explained to us about the ballet or about my role.' This was not unusual as choreographers never deemed it necessary to explain much to dancers – imagine actors learning the words of a play without knowing the plot? Unthinkable now, but dancers of the past were not expected to think.

There grew up a kind of underground movement in that basement studio, a conspiracy to keep Mim out. It is probable that Agnes, a frustrated dancer herself, stoked the fires of resentment against Rambert. It smacked of ingratitude and Rambert would not have expected this, only recognition of her artistic integrity and experience. She was too outspoken and at times lacked dignity, something she only acquired in old age. Meanwhile she was treated like an outcast in her own theatre. It was a case of 'biter gets bitten'. Much later in her life, she received a loving letter from Tudor who had always appreciated her but at the time could not cope with her. When Rambert died, Agnes, now crippled from a massive stroke, wrote an extravagant letter to Lulu lauding Rambert's talents and character.

CHAPTER 17

During an interview for the 50th anniversary of her company, Rambert told Peter Williams, the dance critic, that she never thought of the future. 'The present always escapes me and only the past remains. Somehow when it's all past, it seems something has been done. But neither at the moment when it was being done did I realise what I did, nor can I think of the future, it's absolutely beyond me.'

Unlike de Valois, who had a vision and worked and planned to create a great ballet company, Rambert did not expect to found a permanent ballet company, she planned only from day to day. She had no ambition to become a latter day Diaghilev and would have thought that presumptuous. But her dancers thought otherwise, they assumed that they were working in order to establish a permanent company. There were short seasons, no longer than two or three weeks. Already in 1935 she was having to seek permission to present her own dancers for the three-week season at the Duke of York Theatre in the West End, when several of her soloists appeared 'by permission' of Lilian Baylis and other theatre directors.

Arnold Haskell wrote a glowing introductory note in the programme. 'The Rambert Ballet in its spirit is Russian Ballet in the finest sense of the word – for here dancing comes first and foremost. They have copied no one, they are themselves important figures in the brilliant renaissance of Ballet that is taking place all over the world today.' Certainly Rambert still had the strongest of her dancers and choreographers, Pearl Argyle, Maude Lloyd, Ashton, Tudor, Gore, Frank Staff, the classical Mary Skeaping and Peggy van Praagh were brilliant technicians and Kyra Nijinsky a distinguished guest artist. Yet surely the most important element was the imaginative choreography, a repertoire produced with artistic taste and integrity, inspired by Rambert herself. Good dancers would come and go during the entire history of the company but it was the repertoire that was so unique, a repertoire that has sadly disappeared over the years. Maybe some of the ballets would have dated but there were others well worth preserving and performing. Ashton's *Les Masques* for instance, to Poulenc's sophisticated music and with stunning black-and-white costumes and décor by Fedorovitch was certainly as outstanding as *Façade* which entered the repertory of the Royal Ballet. And surely more of Tudor's work could have been negotiated and preserved? Costumes got lost or simply fell to bits, scenery and even the original designs were dispersed. The remarkable Elisabeth Schooling restaged one or two of the original productions on film. But so many treasures simply vanished. Is there a more profligate and in some cases extravagant waste of productions than in the world of ballet?

As a student dancer I took part in the first of many seasons at the Birmingham Repertory Theatre in 1936. I was thrilled to be performing in a proper theatre on a proper stage. Little more than an inexperienced schoolgirl, I took part in eleven of the repertoire of twenty-two ballets. I had never worked so hard and revelled in it, even the yells of Rambert coaching me in the *Swan Lake pas de trois* did not dampen my enthusiasm. Bullied and cajoled by Rambert I learnt more in two weeks than I might have learnt in two years in another company. But it was all over so soon. Breathless, exhausted, I had picked up the scent, the excitement of performance. I burst into tears on the platform of Liverpool Street Station as I watched the company dispersing to their homes. My mother, who had been in charge of the wardrobe, looked at me in surprise, a blubbering fourteen year old whose dream had been snatched away from her. 'But darling, you'll see them all again on Monday morning in the studio', she protested. 'It's not the same', I wailed. And indeed, it was not the same. I was expressing a disappointment, a frustration that was to run through the Rambert dancers right up to the moment when in the forties a permanent company came into existence.

There was another three-week season in 1937 at the little Duchess Theatre in Covent Garden. The inadequate technical running of the show marred the success of this season. Perhaps more than any of the other theatrical arts, ballet relies on atmosphere and illusion; the audience feast their eyes on movement, their ears on music. The onlooker is transported into fantasy, a kind of dream world when the imagination harnesses the spirit. Break this magic thread by mundane accidents in the presentation and the spell is broken.

The Birmingham Rep was under the firm directorship of Sir Barry Jackson and being a permanent company the stage staff were efficient and experienced. This apparently was not the case at the Duchess. Rambert's stage manager was Tudor, in between dancing himself. His assistant was John Andrewes, also one of the dancers. Her business manager, who also acted as her private secretary, was an amateur enthusiast, hardly up to the hard edge of the West End Theatre. Either from parsimony or simply lack of funds Rambert tried to run things with a skeleton staff and poor equipment. Corners were cut, the flimsy Ballet Club scenery did not fit, even fell over, the lighting was capricious and the sound system poor and unreliable. Whenever there was a hitch, Mim would emerge between the curtains and in a characteristic gesture ingratiatingly clasping her hands as though in prayer she would plead for the audience's indulgence. Her occasional appearances on stage to make announcements was part of the charm of the Ballet Club, but the door-step trade of the Duchess Theatre was not charmed. It was amateurish, unfair on the hard working dancers, particularly the unique repertory. They deserved better.

Rambert in those early days of contact with the professional theatre was not entirely at her ease, had she been asked she would probably have admitted that she was frightened. She had a homing instinct for the security of the Mercury where as Queen Boss she was in her element. Although she was not a control freak she felt happiest amongst her own family of artists. The confines of the tiny stage did not bother her since she did not have to dance on it. This was the incubator where she could nurture dance as an expressive art form and not simply an entertainment. And there was something of the émigrée's pride of possession, this was her territory, and her home, husband and children were just round the corner. There was a lot of clannishness around the Mercury and a kind of conceit that Rambert dancers were different and special. They had a dangerous sense of superiority that was a poor preparation for life in the larger ballet scene that was to blossom during the war years. The love/hate relationship with Mim bound the company together in a web the threads of which were difficult to break. Ashley with his caustic wit called it 'a *nostalgie de côterie*.'

In a strange theatre she felt vulnerable, and could not cope with managerial issues, box-office problems, stage staff who were unused to temperamental outbursts. In spite of all these difficulties it was during this season that Tudor finally produced his *Dark Elegies* which was eventually recognised as a masterpiece.

At the end of these short seasons or sometimes single performances the dancers returned disconsolate to the confines of the Mercury. It was as though they had experienced the freedom of the bird let out of the cage only to find themselves back again. The freedom was of movement, the opportunity to expand, to stretch, to leap without the constant admonitions of Rambert, 'Not so strong!' 'Look, you are taking up too much space!' 'Don't make faces – don't open your mouth when you are dancing, you look like a cod on a slab!' '*No*, smaller, smaller.'

She always emphasised the importance of keeping your mouth closed with the corners up, and certainly a dancer should not be caught gasping for breath and she considered that the open mouth robbed the face of expression. Another constant cry was 'look up', in other words don't look at the audience, let them look at you. At the Mercury this was doubly important since if you did not look over their heads you met the front row eyeball to eyeball. Dedicated as she was to beauty in all its forms she wisely counselled her dancers in cultivating and preserving their good looks. One day when in the throes of one of her gruelling barre exercises I frowned in an agonising effort to get my leg higher, she came up to me and laying the palm of her little hand on my forehead said, 'Don't spoil your alabaster brow darling.' I never forgot that.

Were there any conferences between Mim and her husband and advisors (if any), as to the future of the newly named Ballet Rambert? It is doubtful, Ashley was immersed in his productions at the Mercury, particularly the presentation of T.S.Eliot's *Murder in the Cathedral*. He spent an increasing amount of time abroad, watching theatre, meeting interesting people, wining and dining. Mim, it seems, no longer had any time to accompany him.

Tudor broke away from Mim after the Duchess season to form his own company. Mim was furious and blamed Agnes for instigating the move. She was probably quite right, Agnes had ambitions of her own, perhaps to 'out-Rambert Rambert?' She organised the first appearance of Tudor and his ballets in Oxford along with her own recital work. Antony bided his time and found her useful but in due course she was jettisoned as being too powerful, another Mim from whom he had escaped. In 1982 Agnes wrote to Lulu, 'I see Antony and Hugh from time to time, and believe it or not, they have with age become gentle and kind.'

Meanwhile the next Birmingham Rep season was imminent. Several of Rambert's key dancers had left with Tudor, Maude Lloyd and Peggy van Praagh among them, and of course Hugh. Fortunately Frank Staff, as handsome as Hugh and a better dancer, was there to replace him but the entire repertoire had to be rehearsed. Maude was the only one who returned to perform with the Ballet Club. Two world class choreographers had moved on, but Rambert had their ballets which formed the foundation stones of a volatile ballet company which in spite of set-backs refused to die.

A tour of the casinos of the south of France cheered everybody up including Mim herself although it did nothing to further the reputation of the company. The Casino theatres were delightful but ballet was regarded as light entertainment by the French clientele, a mere diversion after dinner, so the small repertory had likewise to be light and entertaining. The evening always started with *Les Sylphides*, that much exploited oeuvre of Fokine, although Rambert's version was always charming. *Bar* and *Foyer* would meet with great approval but one wonders whether Andrée's sombre *Death and the Maiden* was a popular choice.

Ashley had warned against the enterprise. The continental theatre world has always been beset with impresarios of dubious reputation, there was and still is a long tradition of small troupes of dancers stranded without the price of their ticket home. Ashley was suspicious of the woman who offered a beguiling tour of the Casino theatres of France and considered her 'shady'. But in spite of these warnings the company went ahead because to Mim the prospect of touring her beloved France was irresistible. She took some of the younger members with her including Sally Gilmour and Walter Gore, who were in the throes of a passionate love-affair, as indeed were Elisabeth Schooling and Frank Staff who subsequently married. Mim approved of love affairs, the Russians thought that sexual experience deepened dancers' expressiveness, and indeed the men of the Ballet Russes, not surprisingly, were at pains to promulgate this theory to innocent new recruits of the company. Mim had a romantic, old-fashioned view of passion which was a quality she appreciated in dancers but in this matter she would certainly not have been so tactless as to lecture her young dancers on the desirability of sexual experience – in any case it would have to be love. She was scornful of 'arid' women and even her teachers were expected to have a private life, she didn't like those who devoted themselves exclusively to teaching.

She wanted to take her daughters to France since both girls were dancing in the company. But Lulu was under age, in any case Ashley put his foot down declaring roundly that 'He did not want his daughters leered at by bearded Frenchmen!' One can't help wondering if he did not refer to them as 'Frogs!' The girls were left mournfully waving to the departing train on Victoria station. To make up for their disappointment they were packed off to Dymchurch with Renee for a week – no substitute for a glamorous tour of French casinos.

Ashley's warnings were well founded, the 'shady lady' disappeared with all the takings and the telegraph wires between France and England buzzed with requests for Daddies to send funds to rescue their pretty daughters from a fate worse than death. Felicity Watt recalled that her parents turned up and whisked her away to safety. Mim must have been given a bad time by Ashley on her return.

One thing this episode does illustrate is Rambert's lack of business acumen in not engaging a sharp-minded business manager to deal with company matters. This particular debacle was not too serious but a far more dramatic scenario developed on the Australian tour of the company and almost resulted in the total demise of Ballet Rambert.

Rambert loved touring, at no time did she feel more part of her company than when she was sharing train calls and even digs with members of her 'band of wanderers'. She possessed all the qualities that her friend Colette wrote about in *La Vagabonde*. 'Rugged health, unshakeable good humour, nerves not worn to a frazzle' (she wore other people's nerves to a frazzle but not her own!) 'A well regulated digestive system... the fatalism that turns a theatrical company... into a caravan of pilgrims... a faith that leads them on from station to station toward the goal never attained... repose.'

Tudor launched his new company with some success at the Westminster Theatre where he shared the programme with de Mille and where he premiered *The Judgment of Paris*. This would have been a perfect ballet for the Mercury and indeed it was acquired by Ballet Rambert later on. It had all the sophistication and wit so endemic to the Ballet Club. The roles of the three prostitutes vying with each other to gain the favour of the drunken client were masterpieces of characterisation tailor-made for each dancer. To watch Agnes, wearing an outrageous 'Baby Doll' wig, her generous bosom encased in a pink satin corselet, a huge bow on her bottom, walking across the stage on bowed legs and high heels was sheer joy. She performed her seduction number, climbing in and out of a hoop with sardonic humour and never moving a muscle of her face. Charlotte Bidmead, an unexceptional Rambert dancer in whom Tudor had devined a dramatic quality, played the thin, depressed, hungry-eyed tart despondently waving her moth-eaten feather boa under the nose of the drunk collapsing on the table. Therese Langfield, the prettiest of the three, leered coyly over a large feather fan. The concept and the designs for this piece were by Hugh. How fascinating it must have been for those early Tudor dancers to devise these characters. The long, sometimes arduous process of having a role created for you is a rare privilege, the participation in the creation of a dance character has an excitement never matched by learning a role already created by another.

Andrée's *Lady into Fox* was a classic example of this. Produced at the Mercury in 1939 it gave Sally Gilmour, now a mature artist, the role of her life. I never saw another dancer in the role nor wanted to. Sally could have made a fine actress and yet words would have added nothing to her interpretation of the trapped animal inside the respectable young Mrs Tebrick of David Garnett's novel. John Drummond has written that the art of ballet was 'entirely successful in suggesting emotion and the intensity of human and superhuman relationships'. Sally Gilmour, by no means a brilliant technician, had a strange quality that everyone called fey even in her everyday life and it was this very quality that gave an intensity to her portrayals of dramatic roles. This would later be brought out by Walter Gore in such works as *Confessional* and indeed although technically she may not have come up to the role of *Giselle* her reading of the mad scene was most moving. *Lady into Fox* created quite a sensation at the time and established Sally as a truly Rambert dancer.

Andrée took *Fox* to America at the outbreak of the war, but it did not appeal to the American audiences, neither did *Death and the Maiden*. This highlights the drawbacks of ballets created by and for one dancer, in the case of *Death* the dancer was Andrée herself whose light, almost ethereal style perfectly suited the role and in both cases the very intimacy of the Mercury Theatre created the right atmosphere. It is quite understandable that a large theatre would have weakened the intensity and the audience's involvement in both these works.

Rambert looked for beauty in her dancers. Tudor chose his dancers for their character and indeed they were neither particularly good-looking nor good dancers, the exception being Maude Lloyd, who was Antony's muse. When de Mille became famous as a choreographer herself, she too tended to choose oddities rather than raving beauties and fitted the role on whatever singular characteristics they had regardless of whether they were the right shape or attractive.

Mim had hoped that Walter Gore would be her next choreographic discovery, but she was disappointed in his first efforts – he was still rather immature – and it was not until after the war that he made his name as a choreographer. She also encouraged Frank Staff, with better results. A reticent young man, Frank had been well trained in South Africa and knew his classical vocabulary. With both musicality and a dry sense of humour, he produced some good work, including in 1939 *Czernyana*, a delightful humorous ballet which brought out all the special qualities of the Rambert dancers. Humour in ballet is rare, most dancers themselves have a natural gift of comedy but few choreographers manage to bring it out. Yet Ashton's sophisticated wit and that of Mim, Ashley and the Ballet Club audience must have rubbed off on these dancers.

Rambert's school and performances continued to run until the declaration of war brought to a close Rambert's finest and unique achievement, and probably the happiest moments of her life. But then that could be said of many people's lives at that time.

CHAPTER 18

The thirties were difficult times for my mother. Widowed early in her marriage she had struggled to bring up her three children on very little money. Both my brothers went to public school but Tony, the younger one, sensitive and not physically strong, could not stand the bullying and was taken away at fourteen. Our doctor recommended that he should take ballet lessons to build up his physique. After a year's preliminary training he joined me at Rambert's. He was exceptionally handsome and well proportioned, but while he might have made a good actor, even a film star, he was not all that interested in ballet, and my mother had to use a great deal of persuasion to get him into class. He sometimes truanted, hotly tracked down by Rambert. He was not naturally loose in the hip-joint and like Billy Chappell found the training physically arduous – and painful. Rambert never bullied him and he accepted her with good humour, except on one occasion. One day he came home complaining of pain in the groin, it appeared that during the barre work Mim had suddenly seized his raised leg in an endeavour to force the dreaded 'turn-out'. Our mother was furious and the next day she marched into Tony's class, took Mim aside, thoroughly told her off and kept Tony away until the injury was healed.

Rambert was not the only teacher to be guilty of what to the layman would seem like brutality. Anatomy was not a requisite subject for the teachers of that generation and Rambert would not have studied it, she knew aesthetically how the body should look but not necessarily how to achieve that look, either the leg was up or it was down, the foot pointed or not, if the line of the position was wrong the pupil was prodded and pushed until the desired effect was achieved, never mind the limitations of the body, she considered hard work would change it. To a certain extent she was right as long as she didn't enforce it on a stiff, English teenage boy.

In spite of my brother's reservations about taking up a career in ballet he endured the training and what he may have lacked in technique was compensated for by height, good looks and a charming personality. Having paid his dues in the Ballet Club performances he went on to join the Markova-Dolin company and Tudor's London Ballet at Toynbee Hall and at the Arts Theatre.

Although our fees were provided for my mother still had to house, clothe and feed us. We were always moving, from house to flat, flat back to house, according to our fluctuating finances but by 1934 the shortage of money had become quite serious. It was during this period that mother took over the wardrobe at the Mercury and Rambert, sympathetic to her difficulties, after a consultation with her husband offered us a maisonette above the row of shops (the theatre site in waiting) at a nominal rent. My mother was grateful for Mim's help although it did put her under an obligation. However, she had no option but to accept what was almost a lifeline.

In some ways it was handy for us to live opposite the Mercury but of course there was a snag in that my mother in particular was too accessible and there was a constant stream of dancers coming for fittings; there were frantic calls for her to hurry over if there were a crisis and Rambert popped in at inconvenient moments and regardless of the work in progress demanded my mother's sole attention. My mother's Christian name was Grace but she was always called Mrs Kelly, even by her closest friends who sometimes abbreviated it to simply Kelly. Rambert alone called her Grace. In the forties, when Grace Kelly became a star, my mother was frequently in receipt of quirky phone calls. Since no one called her by her Christian name, if a man's voice on the phone asked, 'Is that Grace?' she knew immediately that this was a 'rogue' call and her invariable response was 'This is Scotland Yard!'

Rambert's incursions on my mother's quiet moments at the end of the day were tiresome but she understood the intensity of Mim's dedication. Rambert was not considerate of people's privacy, if she had some urgent business that was all that mattered. These visits were an intrusion out of official hours but it never occurred to Mim that she might be unwelcome. Mim herself could not even hold a needle, never mind sew, but somehow her personality and charm overrode all other considerations and mother could never refuse an urgent request and of course she was learning the impromptu nature of the theatre for herself.

'Grace, could you *possibly* let out this bodice for that wretched S... she's got so *huge*, but there is no one to replace her. And this skirt, could you let it down, A... is getting so tall.' Putting on weight or growing tall was a personal affront to Rambert and her grasp of English was sometimes extraordinary. 'She's getting so stout!' This was an expression seldom heard other than from elderly aunts. When in my forties I went on a stringent diet she came up to me and said, 'I'm so glad you have lost weight, I had thought, what a pity Brigitte is getting thick.'

Tony and I under protest sometimes helped our mother. On one occasion she begged us to carry a skip of Agnes de Mille's costumes across the road to the Mercury where she was giving her recitals. Agnes in one of her books refers to Tony and myself as 'Mrs Kelly's two healthy children who had been sold into slavery', which annoyed me greatly. I don't know what she meant but if anyone was a slave it was my mother, not us. Eventually we moved to a flat in Portobello Road where we could breathe more freely although my mother remained devoted to Rambert.

By 1937 the Rambert School was well known and the reputation of Marie Rambert as a person of integrity and dedication attracted talented and interesting people, not only dancers who wished to train, but designers, composers, aspiring choreographers.

The school in the late thirties was a thriving organisation which, though not run as a business nevertheless more than paid for the enterprises of Ashley Dukes and the investment in the buildings that comprised the Mercury. The place hummed, at times almost exploded with activity throughout the day. The professional classes were at eleven in the morning, Rambert's in the main studio, another in the basement studio taken by another teacher. The standard was mixed, members of the company and aspirants upstairs, lesser mortals downstairs or kept to the back of the class. The studio was pretty full, every inch of space was occupied at the barre. If the sweat was not pouring off you by the end of the barre-work Mim considered you had not worked hard enough. Billy Chappell in his book *Studies in Ballet* written in 1948 while serving in the army, gave a graphic and amusing description of class-work. 'In the stuffy overheated air of the rehearsal room, air that after half an hour is thick with the odour of sweating humanity, everything seems to enhance the feeling that "I am here for eternity, painfully trying to turn my legs out. This is my life for the rest of time."' This was particularly so with Mim's barre which seemed to last for ever. Billy, who hated training, wrote 'The barre work is a bore. The centre practice a torture. The adagio a tottering misery. There is a faint lightening of gloom when one reaches the elevation steps for one suddenly realises that the end is in sight.' He adds that the advantages of taking class in the morning are obvious. 'If one feels liverish or splenetic the exercise has a tonic effect and it can certainly be recommended as a drastic but certain antidote to a hangover, a symptomatic state less common in the ballet world than might be imagined.'

When it came to work in the centre the 'lesser mortals' had to keep clear of the star performers charging across the studio and were yelled at by

Mim if they got in the way. Sometimes the outrageousness of her remarks were alleviated by the sheer humour of this impertinent woman.

'You have a bottom like the Hanging Gardens of Babylon', she commented to Ashton, who could not suppress a laugh in spite of the insult. If a dancer was putting on weight she would stand next to her, wrinkle up her nose in distaste and mutter loudly 'Huge' at the same time prodding the poor victim in the waist.

'You are dancing like a great heavy cow, forget the grass and get off the ground', was another spicy shot thrown at Diana Gould, who did not laugh.

'Get out of the way', she would shriek at a poor girl who had stumbled on a step across the floor. Did she realise how abominably rude she was being? Sometimes hurtfully personal? She would never have got away with it in her own country. It was such a shock to her polite English pupils that at first it left them speechless, but eventually they accepted being abused rather as soldiers accept the insults of their sergeant major on the barrack square. They got used to it and could not resist a giggle when she said something really witty.

Occasionally Rambert's conscience smote her and in an endeavour to be fair she reversed the lines of dancers, placing the stars at the back, but if an important visitor appeared to watch there was a hasty reshuffle. This certainly did nothing to boost those dancers' self-confidence but they accepted the situation with humility. There were a few who never quite forgave Mim's tongue and would leave at the end of their training with bitterness in their hearts.

The basement studio retained the atmosphere of below stairs when it had been the kitchen of the house, even to the original sink in the scullery and in the studio itself, another one of those huge 'donkeys' devouring coke in order to provide some semblance of a hot-water system. This studio was really only suitable for the little children's classes for the ceiling was depressingly low and inhibited any effort at jumping high lest one knocked oneself out. A Cecchetti syllabus teacher coached students for their exams in the afternoons downstairs while Mim took her children's class upstairs. The curriculum by today's standards was meagre. There were no classes in any subject other than classical ballet, no *pas de deux*, no character classes and no classes in composition or choreography. When one looks at the variety of subjects taught in today's schools it is surprising how quickly we adapted to other styles once we left to earn our living, but from my own experience in the Russian Ballet I have to say that I had some anguishing moments when I first joined. Leon Woizikovsky was particularly shocked that I had not been taught the mazurka. Mim, however, had coached me in the waltz from *Sylphides* quite beautifully which so impressed Leon that he gave it to me immediately on my arrival in the company.

The pay for teachers and pianists was derisory by today's standards but it was known as a luxury profession and only people who were prepared to go hungry for their art joined in. There were long unpaid holidays and it was run on the old theatrical tradition of 'No play, no pay.' There were many devoted souls who worked tirelessly at the Mercury for love of the arts or simply out of admiration for the people there, they enjoyed being part of the atmosphere. Renee Dukes would not have been paid and indeed probably put her hand into her own pocket on many occasions.

Once my mother started to help out with the wardrobe she found herself gradually drawn in to an atmosphere that she adored, and of course could keep an eye on my brother Tony and me. Eventually she took over the wardrobe, a cubby-hole in the dreaded basement where dancers and Rambert herself would come and confide their troubles to Mrs Kelly's patient and sympathetic ear. She also helped the principals to dress for the Sunday night performances and delighted particularly in the wit of Ashton and Chappell. Fred was very vain and insisted that she sewed him into his sleek black trousers for the Dago in *Façade*.

Since the wardrobe room was located right next to the downstairs studio it was inevitable that the sounds of horrific rows between Hugh and Antony would seep through the thick wall and when the victim was Mim herself she would hurl herself into the quiet atmosphere of the wardrobe to pour out her frustrations to my mother. With her fine nose for divining talent she had discovered that my mother was a gifted interpreter of design and really set her on the path of a new career. Rambert would beg discarded ball gowns off the rich ladies who attended the performances and my mother would take them to pieces and turn Lady Astor's Schiaparelli creation into an equally stunning ballet costume.

Rambert was tireless in her efforts to improve her knowledge of the classical technique, a knowledge that had been denied her at an age when she should have been receiving serious training. She could often be spied in the empty studio of the Mercury before the children's class at four o'clock working with her great friend the beautiful Cleo Nordi, a favourite pupil of Cecchetti. Mim was receiving a lesson at the barre, facing Nordi, together going through the exercises and Nordi giving her corrections. They were an odd couple, Nordi tall, of classical features, her hair parted in the middle Pavlova fashion and drawn down and back to a chignon at the nape of the neck, her beautiful arched foot carefully going through *battements tendus, battements frappés, petits battements sur le coup de pied*, Mim desperately manipulating her foot around these precise exercises. The diminutive Mim worked feverishly wearing the familiar awful baggy tights, tatty pink tutu and worn old pointe shoes. The contrast between the two women was almost grotesque to the eyes of the little pupils peeping round the door of the dressing room waiting for their class.

Nordi had been a member of Anna Pavlova's company and had worshipped the great dancer. She once related how in *Les Sylphides* when the corps de ballet reclined on the floor in static position during the *grand pas de deux*, she, Nordi had almost fainted when Pavlova brushed past her on her exit. A follower of spiritualism, she believed that Pavlova was a member of the spirit world returned in the form of a great dancer. When Angela began to teach at the Mercury Rambert would beg her daughter to give her a class, a request which was not always greeted with enthusiasm bearing in mind the unkindness of her mother during her own training.

Rambert's lifetime exultation in turning cartwheels was quite extraordinary and since she would turn them at the most unexpected and inappropriate moments caused her family, particularly her daughters, painful embarrassment. I once asked her why she enjoyed turning herself upside down. She clasped her hands in ecstasy, 'Oh! It's an expression of freedom, it clears the brain, and the whole world turns with you.'

'Aren't somersaults just as good?'

'Oh no, somersaults, rolly pollies, all those are tricks and demeaning,' she said contemptuously. 'Cartwheels involve the legs, the whole body, the balance.'

If she'd just confined her cartwheels to the dance studio she would not have incurred disapproval from the more straight-laced of her friends. But she was not aware that she was behaving in an embarrassing manner – or perhaps simply not concerned. Could it have been also a way of kicking over the traces, thumbing her nose at the world and of course attracting attention? In her memoir she happily relates how she turned cartwheels all around the outside of the National Gallery. Odd as this behaviour was, it was even more so when in her sixties and wearing a long skirt she attended a reception in the British Embassy on her last visit to Russia. Politicians, bankers, economists stood around glasses in hand solemnly talking business. Presumably Rambert was bored, besides, no one was paying her any attention, so she turned a cartwheel. Amid the general amusement a Russian official who happened to be standing next to her company manager asked;

'That lady? She is Jewish – no?' Embarrassed, her manager nodded.

'Ah! Yes, of course.' To the Russian, this seemed to be a perfectly logical explanation.

In moments of stress she would disappear and be found standing on her head. She said it cleared the brain and calmed her down. Perhaps Paul Dukes had encouraged the habit?

Elisabeth Schooling related how when the company was on tour in the forties there was an almighty row because Mim installed herself in the star dressing-room at stage level and the rest of the company were given dressing-rooms on the next floor up. The hard working dancers had a lot of quick changes of costume and make-up and would have to rush up and down the stairs from the stage.

Elisabeth Schooling plucked up the courage to confront Rambert, telling her roundly that she had no need of a dressing-room since she was not performing herself, and certainly not the star dressing-room. Rambert threw one of her screaming tantrums, then rushed to a paper basket standing in the corner of the room, and plunged her head inside it, one supposes the nearest she could get to actually standing on her head. After a short while she withdrew her head, straightened herself up and beat a dignified retreat – upstairs.

The Rambert dancers and students were in great demand during the latter part of the thirties. As well as the principals taking part in the Sadler's Wells company they became a regular feature of the Opera season at Covent Garden. Whether actually dancing, waving palms in *Lohengrin* or throwing paper flowers in the path of a diva this was enormous fun for which they received the princely sum of twelve shillings and sixpence per performance – a great advance on the five shillings for dancing at the Ballet Club. In the summer, members of the Ballets Russes made guest appearances prior to their own season and danced alongside the admiring Rambert students giving them an invaluable experience denied them once the Royal Ballet took over. Tudor choreographed the dances and almost exclusively used Rambert trained people, a tradition that came to a halt at the outbreak of the war. The dancers also took part in films, sometimes merely as extras which they rather snootily accepted being in need of the cash. H.G. Wells's *Things to Come* was a memorable example. Pearl Argyle was one of the stars and loyally procured crowd work for half the school. It was one of my first jobs and turned out to be a depressing experience during a particularly cold winter. Dressed in short rubber tunics, bare legs and open-toed sandals we spent days rushing up an enormous flight of steps cheering. The path from dressing-room to studio was through alleys of deep, icy mud.

Mugs of hot Bovril were served in a tent on the Denham Studios lot in spite of which the entire cast went down with heavy colds.

In 1936 Ballet Rambert, then called the Mercury Ballet, took part in the very first television transmission of ballet, three days after the initial launch of the station from Alexandra Palace. 'The programme on that occasion consisted of solos and short extracts from eight ballets.' The dancers were Maude Lloyd, Walter Gore, Andrée Howard, Frank Staff, Hugh Laing, Elisabeth Schooling, Deborah Dering, Suzette Morfield and myself aged fifteen. I danced the Sugar Plum Fairy solo from *Casse Noisette*. Thrilled as I was to be included in such a novel and fascinating experience I was dismayed to be told I had to keep within a space the size of a pocket handkerchief. Heavily made-up with a bright orange foundation I was yelled at by Rambert whenever I 'overspilled' the white boundary tape stuck to the floor. Blinded by the lights I could not see the tape and danced the whole solo looking down with Mim bawling out her usual admonition to 'Look up and corners of the mouth up!'

Huw Wheldon was the charismatic director, a tall hawk-nosed man who managed Mim and the dancers with charm and firmness. The two announcers were Jasmine Bligh and Elizabeth Cowell, beautiful, well-groomed and who spoke with such exaggerated upper-class accents that they would today be greeted with hoots of laughter. The most memorable thing about this experience was that we were able to dash to an adjoining studio and watch ourselves perform.

The last tour of the existing Rambert dancers took place in August 1939 when they performed in Dublin. They spent a happy summer at the Mercury where the company was now well established and, in spite of defections, still producing new ballets foremost of which was *Fox* which owing to popular demand was included at each performance. Both dancers and audience seemed impervious to the imminence of war or perhaps with typical British stoicism they preferred to ignore it. Dancers are not political creatures, cocooned as they are in their own singular way of life. Daily classes, rehearsals, performances swallow up the mental and physical energy and there is no room for the realities of life outside the studio. Some dancers are unaware to the point of stupidity, like the young de Basil dancer who turned up in Berlin to join the company in September 1939 blissfully unaware that the war had started. He got out by the skin of his teeth.

Eight years of hard and dedicated work had produced a remarkable cornucopia of original ballets. 'Rambertism' was now firmly established. As Rambert herself put it many years later, 'We are to the Royal Ballet what the Tate is to the National Gallery', a clever analogy and one which at the time must have been hard to concede. She never voiced her disappointment at not having her own full-sized theatre opposite the Mercury although there must have been bad moments when she reproached her husband for not pushing forward his plans and refusing to accept financial help to build it.

The Second World War curtailed and almost killed an enterprise that might have developed with the building of a theatre into a centre of drama and ballet that would have made a unique and exciting contribution to the cultural arts in England. Ironically it was the opportunities of the war years that made possible the achievement of Ninette de Valois's ambitions for her company while Rambert's contribution to the future of ballet in this country was almost eclipsed. The Sadler's Wells Ballet company moved into the Royal Opera House whilst Rambert and her company were relegated to touring the provinces, struggling to survive in the face of growing competition.

CHAPTER 19

Although once she had left Poland Mim had little contact with her relatives, on the occasion in 1935 when she visited Russia she stopped over in Warsaw on her return journey. She began to take an interest in a niece who was taking ballet lessons. Hania was almost a replica of Mim herself, except that she had a sweeter, gentler temperament. She related how much she was in awe of her famous aunt. 'This great lady from England', who eyed her and said 'Show me an arabesque.' Hania did her best. Rambert seemed satisfied and subsequently sent money from England to pay for her lessons. Eventually Hania came to the Mercury where she trained to be a teacher. She adored her aunt and saw a side of her that was kind and loving, a side to Rambert's complicated nature that her company only occasionally glimpsed.

Although in 1939 no one quite knew what had been happening in Germany there had been a steady influx of Jewish émigrés throughout the thirties and these people provided enough evidence of Adolph Hitler's fanatical hatred of the Jewish race. It is reasonable to suppose that Ashley Dukes, once war was declared on September 3, was aware of the delicate situation where his wife was concerned. Whether Mim herself was frightened of Hitler is uncertain, but she was certainly afraid of bombs. She was to learn much later that members of her family who had not emigrated to Israel had died in the gas-chambers of Auschwitz.

Once war was declared parents pleaded with Rambert to evacuate the school to a safe place in the country. Louis Behrends and his wife offered to house the school in their large house and grounds in Burghclere near Newbury. The Behrends were from a cotton manufacturing background in Egypt, interesting people, very rich and great patrons of the arts. In 1933 they had built a chapel in the grounds of their house especially to house the work of Stanley Spencer, the artist. The Behrends had seen Spencer's work in 1923 when he exhibited a set of drawings showing the interior of a small chapel whose side walls were divided up into panels. Each of the panels, sixteen of them in all, was worked out in firm detail as though the whole interior of this imagined building had taken final shape in the artist's mind. Realising that here was a man with an urgent message to communicate the Behrends built the chapel that Spencer had seen in

Frederick Ashton at Dymchurch, imitating La Nijinska.

Mim showing off in lifts partnered by Sir Paul Dukes.

Dymchurch

Lulu in the 'fish dive' partnered by Frank Staff.

Elisabeth Schooling, Ann Gee, Olive Sarel, Andrée Howard, Brigitte Kelly, Suzette Morfield, Pearl Argyle in *The Rape of the Lock*.

Angela Ellis teaching a boys' class.

Ballet Rambert in *Coppélia*.

Brigitte Kelly teaching a boys' class.

Ballet Rambert in *La Sylphide*.

Lucette Aldous and Norman Morrice in *Night Shadow*,

Christopher Bruce in *Hazard*.

Pierrot Lunaire.

his imagination. The work was completed in 1933 and Spencer painted all the panels including a huge Resurrection on the main wall.

The Behrends's home, Gray House, was not too far away from London but far enough to avoid the bombs. Louis Behrends and his wife were friends and admirers of the Ballet Club and together with many people who had beautiful homes in the country were alarmed at the prospect of having East End evacuees billeted on them. Infinitely preferable were little ballet students of middle-class background and habits. There is no record of how many pupils there were but Jane Shore (later Nicholas) who was ten years old at the time thinks it was no more than a dozen children since many parents at the outbreak of war sent their children to live with relations in Canada or Australia.

Angela, now nineteen, and Mim arrived at Gray House with Helen the faithful family cook and housekeeper, also a delightful school secretary who had been a silent film star. It was a strange and somewhat alarming invasion for the owners of the house. They were all allocated rooms in which to sleep, sharing, but were not allowed the run of the house. Angela, who hated the whole expedition, had been bulldozed into going as a relief ballet teacher whereas Lulu stayed behind with her father at Campden Hill. Angela shared a room with a student, not with her mother, which tells us something about the relationship.

Ballet lessons were given in a big room with a parquet floor, quite unsuitable for ballet since it was slippery so as a precaution against possible mishaps there was no pointe-work. Angela did most of the teaching while Mim escaped to London. I asked Angela if she was paid for her teaching, 'No, of course not!' she replied, 'What are you thinking of? Rambert – pay?' Mim obviously considered that it was quite enough that she was giving her daughter an opportunity to develop as a teacher. Angela enjoyed her first classes and it launched her into her future career and she eventually took over directorship of the school.

Whatever inconvenience to the Behrends this influx of people caused them it was preferable to Eastenders from London. A large outhouse or perhaps it was a barn was put at the school's disposal where Helen cooked and served meals and there was a sort of common room. The children of course needed academic schooling as well as continuing their ballet training. Fortunately there was a school only a mile away and the little dancers cycled there after breakfast. This unusual influx was eyed with great curiosity by the other pupils, some of whom were evacuees. True to Rambert tradition 'her' children would have been well proportioned, slight and good-looking, quite unlike the average schoolchild, and some noses were put out of joint when the newcomers excelled in gym. Rambert mentions that she overheard two little evacuees discussing a herd of black cows in a field and concluding that they gave black milk. It was a strange environment and a far cry from her hectic London life and it is problematical whether she enjoyed staying with the Behrends but she was adaptable and loved the countryside and perhaps after all those years of tireless endeavour it was a breathing space for her.

It was bitterly cold that winter of 1939 and the children cycled along icy roads, the trees overhead hung with icicles, and some of the trees lying across their path. In the evenings they would sit around the big kitchen table where it was warmer. The French teacher of the school had left precipitately to rejoin her family in France so Mim was asked to replace her. This proved quite a joyous experience for both Mim and the children. Always unorthodox in her ideas, instead of struggling through a French text book, probably of the useless 'plume de ma tante' variety, Mim threw it away, procured from somewhere a gramophone record of the *Marseillaise* and proceeded to teach it to her pupils. The words of the *Marseillaise* are the rousing cry of the revolution and embody all the passion and colour of the French language. How inspiring for the children, how they must have loved their fiery little teacher with the bright black eyes. She continued with records sung by Charles Trenet singing his own compositions, some of them taken from the poems of Jacques Prévert and using a wonderful, expressive vocabulary. Rambert writes that 'Our lessons were very gay, and within two terms French became quite familiar to them.' Those pupils would never forget her, she was indeed unforgettable, capable of rising to a diversity of situations and calling on her fertile imagination to solve problems beyond the capacity of her duller contemporaries.

This reminds me of a moment during the coffee break at the Mercury in the sixties when I had returned to teach. Pianists and teachers took their break in the print room, now the common room with Ashley Duke's famous bar still standing looking rather forlorn and neglected. Rambert often spoke to me in French which delighted me as she spoke it so beautifully. Sitting up at the bar one chilly winter's morning, warming our frozen hands with our mugs of coffee, for some reason we got on to the subject of national anthems. Suddenly Rambert launched with tremendous gusto into the *Marseillaise* backed up by myself with fervour. When it came to the inspiring cry 'Aux armes citoyens!' our astonished audience nearly dropped their coffee cups and we ended with a flourish worthy of true revolutionaries.

The Behrends eventually tired of their guests, they interfered with their lives and Rambert no doubt tired of the herd of black cows. The school dispersed and she returned to London. Ashley and Lulu had stayed on in London and it was a valuable moment when they drew closer to each other, free of the turbulence of Mim's presence. Helen went away to a war job in a factory making munitions, the Campden Hill house had been so cold that Ashley and Lulu had spent the winter in the flat above the Mercury. Lulu recalls they ate out in a restaurant every day.

CHAPTER 20

An eerie silence had reigned over the theatrical world in September 1939 as London waited apprehensively for the bombing to start. People slept fitfully at night ready to spring out into their hastily erected air-raid shelters in the garden or scuttle down to the cellar. Boxes of medicines and provisions stood ready. Many people, following the advice from the BBC, had obediently sealed up the windows of a spare room against gas-attacks, black lugubrious looking stuff blocked out the light at night, brown cardboard boxes housing hideous-looking gas-masks hung in the hall-ways, and everyone carried one in the day-time strung across themselves on string. There were vigils in front of the radio lest the latest news was missed. Sometimes luminous wax gardenias were pinned to lapels worn in the darkened streets to avoid banging into each other. But apart from the drone of Hitler's heavy aircraft flying across the city at night, exercising the 'war of nerves', nothing happened.

People gradually resumed their normal lives, the theatres re-opened and the Rambert dancers, bored with the inactivity, turned up one by one at the Mercury and the daily class was resumed. Ashley Dukes was contemptuous of the people he called *les embusqués* (shirkers) who left the country at the outbreak of war. W.H. Auden, Christopher Isherwood, Tudor, Hugh and Andrée were among those who sailed to America before war broke out.

In the absence of Rambert, Walter Gore offered to take over the reins and backed by Ashley began rehearsals of the repertoire. Mim must have agreed to the arrangement with some reluctance, but in the circumstances she had no option but to acquiesce. She came up to London, watched a rehearsal, criticised the casting and with lips pursed in a characteristic expression of forbearance, said nothing more and went back to her school.

Ashley Dukes produced a translation of a play by Machiavelli at the Mercury. *Mandragola* was a great success and ran for fifty performances during the cold winter months when heavy snow lay on the ground and people shivered miserably in a constant state of tension. There was a great need of diversion and the theatres were packed with patrons willing to trudge in the blacked-out city to the West End. Small ballet companies sprang up like mushrooms after rain, it was an extraordinary moment, suddenly ballet was seen as the perfect escape from reality.

Ashley Dukes was not slow to read the message. In December, Ballet Rambert gave a season at the Duchess Theatre opening with Frank Staff's new ballet *Czernyana*. Frank couldn't have chosen a better moment. It was bright, witty and fun, the décor and costumes by Eve Swinstead-Smith were smart and modern, white and blue. Schooling danced a pert number sniffing a red carnation. Was there perhaps a subtle hint of patriotism in these colours? Certainly it was a relief from the dark dinginess outside of a London without light. The company enjoyed it, revelling in Staff's spoof on different styles of choreography. Frank, a quietly humorous young man, was an able performer but one always had the feeling that he was slightly embarrassed at being a dancer in the days when it was still considered a rather effeminate profession for a man. Perhaps because of this he choreographed with his tongue in his cheek, there was a subtle send-up quality to his approach. Within the choreography of *Czerny*, arranged to the composer's piano pieces, there were some hilarious moments. *Se Habla Espagnol*, a send-up of a Spanish dancer, was performed by Frank himself and the Massine-style symphonic section when the dancers overdid the Central-European modern movements of *Choreartium* and *Les Présages* was extremely witty. Alas that this kind of humour dates and when Schooling reproduced it for a performance of the Rambert School in the seventies neither audience nor dancers understood the witty comments on a 1930s rep.

Mim must have been upset not to have assisted in the production of this ballet although the dancers were probably relieved, they simply got on with their work anxious that the company should survive. They were concerned as much for her as for themselves that the company should remain intact and were in fact fighting for its survival, a fact perhaps not quite appreciated by its originator.

Although the Duchess season was a success, the future of the company was in doubt. Without contracts for permanent employment the dancers simply had to look elsewhere and with the re-opening of the theatres in the West End there was plenty of work to be found, perhaps not always of the highest standard but the experienced dancers that Rambert had produced were much in demand by the newly formed dance companies and also in musicals where they would be well paid. And of course there was the call-up. Many of the best male dancers would in due course disappear into the armed forces. But the winter and spring of the 'war on nerves' when there was an almost unnatural calm provided a unique moment for the emergence of new projects that carried the live theatre to not only every corner of the British Isles but far afield wherever there were troops fighting the war.

G. M. Kelly's reputation as a gifted costumière had grown considerably by 1939, designers appreciated her artistic flair and understanding of their work. Sophie Fedorovitch, Nadia Benois, Billy Chappell and Hugh Stevenson found her a sensitive interpreter of their designs. Hugh, a sweet-tempered, wonderfully gifted artist was a great friend and his early death affected her deeply.

One day in the summer of 1940 she was approached by Oliver Messel, the famous designer, to make the costumes for a production of Jean Cocteau's *The Infernal Machine*, a modernised version of *Oedipus Rex*. This was to be produced at the Arts Theatre Club in Leicester Square. Messel, a designer of exquisite taste, was then at the height of his fame and my mother was thrilled to be asked to be involved with what promised to be a prestigious production. The cast was led by the beautiful Leueen McGrath as the Sphinx, Peter Glenville as the vain, egotistical, petulant young Oedipus and Jeanne de Casalis in the dramatic role of Jocasta. This piece of casting was interesting since de Casalis was famous for her hilarious monologues as Mrs Feather, the dotty lady who got terribly muddled ordering by phone *A Dozen Damask Dinner Napkins*.

We were by then living in a studio flat in Hampstead. The main living room had a glass roof which, once the war had started, turned out to be a most unsuitable dwelling place because of the anti- aircraft guns positioned on the Heath above us. They kept up a nightly barrage aimed at the sinister presence of Nazi bombers relentlessly passing overhead, caught in the searchlights scouring the night sky. The shrapnel hailed down on our glass roof with a deafening noise. In spite of this nightly disturbance my mother made her way across London by bus to Messel's studio flat in Yeoman's Row, off Brompton Road, arriving home exhausted but stimulated by the experience of working in such a fascinating atmosphere.

The sheer glamour of the large studio was dazzling, the effect of entirely white furniture, rugs and walls at a time when white had not yet become fashionable was breathtaking. A staircase worthy of the first appearance of a great star wound down from the gallery where Oliver had his bedroom. I was recruited to pose on this staircase in Jocasta's white robe and crown for a publicity photograph with Peter looking unbelievably handsome in helmet and Grecian armour, Oliver equally stunning in his army officer's uniform. The photograph appeared on the front page of *The Tatler*. At a high point in my career as a dancer I was delighted at the publicity. De

Casalis, understandably, was furious. Why I was called upon to stand in for her I have no idea, but she was apparently a difficult lady.

The studio was crowded with props and objects from past productions, plaster sculptures of cupids; winged angels dangling from the ceiling; body armour sculpted from wire and plaster and a spectacular head, wings and paws of a large plaster Sphinx into which Leueen would have to squeeze herself as the living Sphinx. Standing on its own platform was a large glass case which housed a rather grim full-sized effigy of Elizabeth Tudor's head wearing her crown and a huge lace ruff. Messel was famous for his masks which had been shown at an exhibition in 1925 and these striking masks were hung all around the studio, giving the rather frightening impression that a hundred eyes were staring at you. There were masks of the Furies, of nymphs, of negroes, of Greek gods all made from papier-mâché, an art to which Messel introduced my mother. He also showed her how to make headdresses, tiaras and crowns out of pipe-cleaners wound with silver and gold ribbon on which were stuck or stitched imitation jewels. Hugh Skillen, a brilliant technical designer, had invented, apart from armour, women's breasts, fashioned very realistically from some new kind of plastic material. These breasts lying around amidst a jumble of other props created quite a stir to visitors unused to the eccentricities of theatrical designers.

In one corner of the studio standing on a table was a model of a stage on which Messel demonstrated his designs and décor to a visiting producer. He was brilliantly clever at creating the illusion of theatre and extremely knowledgeable. My mother was dazzled not only by Oliver but also Peter who was his partner and who lived in the flat beneath. Draping himself elegantly on the huge chaise-longue he entertained everyone with his witty dialogue which seemed to pour out of him like a bubbling stream – not so surprising when one remembers that his father was Shaun Glenville, a well known comedian of his time, and his mother was Dorothy Ward, the most famous pantomime principal boy of them all. My mother made her costumes for that year's pantomime and was intrigued by this tall, red-haired woman who couldn't stop talking all through the fittings, revealing the most intimate details of her life. Well into her fifties, and still displaying fabulous legs, she confided that the secret of staying young was to have an active sex life. She had in fact been the mistress of a famous member of the aristocracy for many years and Peter cherished a secret hope that he was in fact this man's son.

The pièce de résistance in Messel's studio in 1940 was a small plasticine model of a naked Adolph Hitler which stood on a table with a box of pins beside it. Visitors were invited to stick a pin into the Fuehrer and, I need hardly add that the carefully sculpted area round the genitals were the most popular.

Messel was by then in uniform in his war-time capacity as head of the camouflage corps having been given leave of absence in order to work on *The Infernal Machine*. A sophisticated and good-looking man he had a delightful personality, spoke in a soft hesitant voice which belied a quite tough professionalism, and he could be kind. Realising my mother's predicament with regard to our living accommodation he was instrumental in obtaining for her one of the little Queen Anne terraced houses that ran along opposite the studios. The entire row had been condemned but were saved from demolition by the outbreak of the war and, again with the influence of Oliver, being classed as ancient monuments, although this did not prevent them from being demolished when the war ended.

We moved in to 23 Yeoman's Row shortly after the start of the Blitz and my mother turned the first floor into workrooms and ran her business with great success for several years. A few years later she was instrumental in helping Fred Ashton to obtain the house next door.

The Infernal Machine opened on 5 September 1940, the night of the first blitz on London. It struggled with empty houses for a week or so but, along with the other London theatres, the Arts Theatre closed down.

A series of lunch-time concerts at the National Gallery had been instigated by the famous pianist Myra Hess and were achieving great success. Office workers and people who worked in the West End queued to snatch a magic hour of listening to virtuoso musicians in the calm atmosphere of a loved building that for all they knew might no longer be there the following morning. There was a strange urgency in people's desire to escape for a fleeting moment the oppressive foreboding that haunted every waking, and indeed sleeping, moment of their lives.

Harold de Vahl Rubin was one of several sharp entrepreneurs who sprang up at the outset of the war and who took advantage of the need of the public for the kind of escapist entertainment that ballet could provide. Rubin was a rich ex-army captain turned impresario who had made his money from sheep farming in Australia. Perceiving that here was an opportunity to cash in on an excellent idea, he decided to emulate the National Gallery and present lunch-time ballet at the Arts Theatre, which he had leased. Diana Gould, rather surprisingly, had been acting as his social secretary enlisted to attract membership of the Arts Theatre. He was to engage three small ballet companies taking it in turn, to perform in the tiny theatre, not that much larger than the Mercury.

Tudor's sudden departure to the USA had left his devoted acolytes in the lurch. His London Ballet had evolved into an unusually interesting company which showed every sign of developing into a major one. In addition to the works created for the Ballet Club he had added several new ballets to the repertoire and attracted an enthusiastic following at Toynbee Hall. The dancers had been carefully chosen to suit Tudor's style and Margaret Craske, the famous Cecchetti teacher, was adviser and teacher for the company. No one was sure whether Tudor would return from New York at the termination of his engagement to Ballet Theatre, so for the time being the company was in abeyance. It seems that Tudor – unbeknown to anyone – had been negotiating throughout the summer with Rubin planning the transfer of the London Ballet to the Arts Theatre. The company was in the charge of Maude Lloyd and Peggy Van Praagh and almost immediately after Tudor's departure Peggy, the more pragmatic of the two, was approached by Rubin, Tudor was contacted and gave his consent to the proposition. Rubin had already set up a small company, the Arts Theatre Ballet, under the directorship of Keith Lester, a former member of the Markova-Dolin company. He now approached Ashley Dukes with the proposition that the Rambert company should join up at the Arts Theatre.

The situation of Ballet Rambert at that moment was precarious. The dancers, kept going by picking up odd commercial dancing jobs or simply not working at all, were depressed. Ashley, who made all the decisions, was unhelpful. To quote Kathrine Sorley Walker, 'He felt that to set up a permanent company, take on touring and extended London seasons would be a very risky business without solid financial backing. When tour dates were proposed therefore, he apparently often asked for the kind of weekly guarantee that was out of the question for provincial theatres to meet.' Sorley Walker continues, 'Some people – he does not seem to have been a popular man, pompous and domineering are adjectives that have been applied to him – suspected that his underlying motive was a reluctance to see his wife outstrip him in theatrical fame. But whether or not this was the case it would have been hard to get for Rambert the kind of backing that had been given to the Markova-Dolin Ballet.'

The absence of visiting foreign companies opened up possibilities for several new English companies which were being formed; there were many excellent dancers available stranded in England by the outbreak of war. The open classes in the West End were attended by strong experienced dancers, soloists, *premier danseurs*, even ballerinas keeping a weather eye on the opportunities that were fast developing. The Rambert company did not come high on that list, it had a special, rather austere reputation, the Rambert dancers were considered aloof.

When Ashley was approached by Rubin it is not surprising that he seized the opportunity to be rid of a responsibility that kept him from concentrating on his own plans. Perhaps he was weary of the vicissitudes of looking after a volatile group of people whom he did not particularly like. The school was one thing, it brought in a useful income, but to have the premises permanently cluttered up by out-of-work dancers must have got on his nerves. He was thankful to assign Ballet Rambert to Harold Rubin – no one knows the details of the agreement but it took three years to wrest the company from the grip of, what seemed at the time, its saviour. To give Ashley Dukes the benefit of the doubt he could not have realised that he nearly lost Ballet Rambert for Mim altogether.

CHAPTER 21

The lunchtime ballet performances at the Arts, although not too gruelling at the start – after all, the performance only lasted an hour – became more arduous as Rubin, having hit on an excellent idea became increasingly greedy and first added another performance, and then yet another teatime performance. The dancers, having taken class at 10 am followed by a rehearsal, snatched cups of coffee and sandwiches while they made up for the first show at 1pm. There was a quarter hour interval between the three performances when the theatre was cleared and cleaned of dog-eared sandwiches and cigarette stubs. The project was undeniably a huge success and the female dancers of all three companies could not but be grateful to be saved from the dreaded call-up. By 1940 this included every woman between the ages of 18 to 45 although entertainment being considered important to keep up the morale of the people, performers were excused National Service, providing they were in work.

The plan was that each company took it in turn to perform at the Arts while the other two toured. Rubin took full advantage of the wartime situation of the dancers and paid them less than the Equity minimum wage, but they were in no position to complain and according to Diana Gould dancers were used to 'slavery' and poor conditions. Fernau Hall wrote in the forties, 'The life of the typical dancer is one of hard work, grinding poverty and personal and artistic frustration!' This is a rather over-dramatised view from a critic who himself perhaps suffered from personal and artistic frustration, but the word 'slavery' frequently appears in the memoirs of dancers. The dictionary's interpretation of the word is 'bondage, servitude'. Artists, the beggars of society, are often, and from choice, slaves to their art, but not as is inferred to overlords but because of the fear of the call-up the 1940s dancers were nearer to that situation than they had ever been or indeed would be again. The mere fact that dancers have always been prepared to put up with financial insecurity and general discomfort illustrates how much they love their occupation in contrast to people trapped in jobs they dislike. Hall did mention one interesting point; 'Until the reforms in the conditions of work of nurses recommended in 1947, the dancers shared with the nurses the unhappy distinction of being

the worst exploited of all professional workers; the eventual reforms left them in a class by themselves.'

The 'Art for Art's Sake' pre-war ethos still prevailed in 1939 and suited Harold Rubin well. Providing the ballets were presented with integrity, and Rambert saw to that, any monetary considerations regarding the 'slave-dancers' was of no consequence and, never having paid her dancers proper salaries at the Mercury, she thought such things secondary to the pursuit of excellence. Along with the London Ballet Rubin acquired two 'ready-made' companies complete with dancers, scenery, costumes and a distinguished repertoire. Only his own 'Arts Theatre Ballet' required him to put his hand into his pocket and he would have been a fool to let this unique opportunity slip through his fingers. The exhausting work, the poor living conditions on tour and the general ad hoc performing situations dancers still find themselves in depicts a life that seems almost intolerable to the average person. But these were young, fit people in their teens and twenties who considered the general life of the theatre an adventure, fun, hilarious at times. A sense of humour was an essential and no one had a greater sense of humour than Rambert herself, it leavened her personality. Dancers share an easy companionship, a mutual interest and at that moment in 1940 felt that they were contributing something special to the lives of ordinary men and women at a time of great anxiety. It was certainly preferable to peeling buckets of potatoes or cleaning out latrines in the women's forces which might have been their fate, untrained as they were in any occupation but their own.

The little Arts Theatre was not really suitable for ballet although the stage was bigger than the Mercury's. There was no backstage or wings to speak of, a very perilous, steep flight of steps led from the first floor straight on to the stage, the dressing-rooms were awful and there was simply not enough room once the two companies had merged, and some of the younger dancers had to be dropped. However, since there was a shortage of men due to the call-up, Robert Harrold, a raw young recruit with a round baby face, joined in the last days at the Arts and recalled that he was literally thrown on, 'without a clue as to what I was supposed to be doing'.

While the London Ballet and the Arts Theatre Ballet took class and rehearsal as best they could on the premises, Mim insisted when they were in London that her company returned to their home base at the Mercury, the heart of Ballet Rambert, for their class, regardless of where they might be working for their bread and butter. The class for the dancer is unique, separate from the life of the actor, the singer, the recitalist, it is the place to which they return from whatever problems, private or professional, they may have endured, a place where they work alongside comrades. Following on to her gruelling class and a hectic rehearsal for whatever ballet was being performed that day, they had to get from Notting Hill Gate to Leicester Square in time to get ready for the show. Mim would not have considered this of any consequence and would hop on to public transport quite happily with members of her company. In her eighties she was still travelling by tube to Covent Garden at night, considering a taxi a gross extravagance. Robin Howard, that good man who was the founder of London Contemporary Dance, hearing of this, arranged for her to have a minicab at her disposal whenever she attended a performance in the West End.

Ballet Rambert, now under the control of Rubin, merged with the London Ballet to the benefit of both companies inasmuch as the repertoire was the richest and most interesting that had ever existed in England.

During the unsettled atmosphere of the 1940s more interesting ballets were created by Staff, Andrée Howard and Walter Gore. Although Rambert herself could not give her time to the company since she was with the school in Berkshire there was still that aura of creativity that seemed part of the fabric of the company. In the absence of Mim, the company was run by the dancers themselves headed by van Praagh and Maude who were now, with the amalgamation, back in their home stable. Andrée, disappointed with her visit to New York, had managed to get herself back to England and returned to produce the best work of her career with *La Fête Ètrange*. Frank Staff produced an enchantingly entertaining ballet to Prokofiev's *Peter and the Wolf*. Faithfully following the storyline, Staff cast it with a perceptiveness of the special qualities of the Rambert dancers, in particular the casting of Lulu as Peter was an inspired choice. The loose-limbed gambling gait that was characteristic of Lu, the flaxen Russian peasant wig highlighting her slightly foreign gamine face and dressed in a Russian peasant style tunic and boots, she personified Peter. Mim nearly burst with pride to see her younger daughter featured in a role that perfectly suited her unusual qualities. Both girls had of course been performing with the company from the moment they left school although Angela was serving her apprenticeship with the school at that particular time. It came hard on her to know that Lu had been given a leading role while she languished in the countryside.

The lunch and tea performances were so popular that Rubin ordered another 'sherry' performance in the early evening that stretched the dancers past endurance. Jubilant at 'his' success he leased the Ambassadors theatre so that he had two companies, and two audiences on the go. Just at that moment when some theatres had closed down because of the Blitz it was no problem to find a venue.

Where did Mim stand in all this ruthless exploitation of her company? Firebrand though she was, she could fight passionately for the survival of her company, but neither she nor Ashley Dukes was a match for this sharp business man, nor for business about which she knew absolutely nothing and indeed for which she had a contempt. She must have been most unhappy but she never dropped her guard where her dancers were concerned, never confided her worries to them, always keeping what the British would call 'a stiff upper lip' although she would not have recognised this phrase. And she could not expect much sympathy from her husband, who to be fair had warned her against having anything to do with a man who was only interested in money,

It couldn't last. By the end of the summer of 1941 the dancers, overworked and scandalously underpaid, refused to continue working under these terms. There were arguments and the normal camaraderie of the company was broken. Dancers are not militant by nature, they are unusually long suffering, but once they become unhappy and restive they will find the courage to strike. Rubin's arrogant posture as a patron of the arts provoked ridicule and infuriated the company. Although he could not interfere artistically with the London-Rambert company, the Arts Theatre ballet was his and he showed his total ignorance of dance by commissioning Elsa Brunelleschi, a teacher and a personal friend of his, to choreograph a Spanish ballet, without consulting the company. Ignoring the experienced dancers, he insisted on starring a new sixteen-year-old recruit straight out of Brunelleschi's school. Rubin had developed a passion for the talented, pretty, but totally inexperienced Sara Luzita. He was old enough to be her father and Sara was embarrassed by the attentions of this arrogant man who chain-smoked Turkish cigarettes which remained in the corner of his mouth even when he was speaking. It was a classic tale of the infatuation of a patron for a dancer which in this case had dramatic consequences. The Spanish ballet was put on hold while the controversy raged and was eventually performed in Birmingham prior to closure. It was an amateurish disaster, the dancers hated it, Rambert who disliked Brunelleschi (the feeling was mutual) was scornful of what was an insult to the high standard of choreography expected by discerning audiences.

The dancers had had enough. They confronted Rubin with a demand for better pay. When Rubin refused, Equity (the actors' union) was called in and there was a meeting between the representatives of each company. The Equity representative formally requested more money for the dancers and, cornered, the defiant Rubin threatened to close down the whole enterprise.

Robert Harrold, although vaguely aware of the turbulence and acrimony, was more concerned with acquitting himself well as a newcomer. One day when he was leaving to go to the theatre Ashley Dukes gave him a letter addressed to Harold Rubin with strict instructions to hand it to him personally. 'At that time I had no idea what was in the letter – no one ever said', Bobby reminisced. He accomplished his mission and did not learn until afterwards that he had handed a writ to Rubin demanding the return of Ballet Rambert to its rightful owners. There are conflicting accounts of this unpleasant episode in the fortunes of Ballet Rambert, and it was not to be the last for there would more mishandling of the business side of the company during the turbulent post-war years. The problem seems invariably to have been Mim's and Ashley's determination to keep matters in their own hands rather than hire the services of a good business manager. Whether this was due to parsimony or simply naiveté is questionable. In this instance Harold Rubin managed to prevent the company from performing again until 1943, claiming that the scenery and costumes had been leased to him up to that time.

Fortunately Rambert at that time had many devoted followers who were resolved not to allow the demise of what was increasingly seen as a milestone in the development of English ballet.

The company dispersed, finding work in the burgeoning wartime musical theatre. This was a dangerous moment for Mim. What would she have done without her company, the motivation of her life? Gone back to being a dutiful wife and mother? It seems that she was not entirely suited to either of these roles. She was 52, not a propitious age to start your life anew. Her husband was taking his own course and that included casting his roving eye away from Mim, although he always kept his eye on her problems; her daughters too had not much need of her, soon they would marry and lead their own lives. There was the school, of course, but she had always been beguiled by the smell of theatre in her nostrils, and had now caught the magic of not only controlling her artists, but being one of them. She needed to be a member of that caravan of nomadic performers. In spite of all the goading and insults her dancers had to endure, they loved her and most of them understood her and did not desert her. They came back to work in class at the Mercury but they only ever made guest appearances and she would have to train a new generation of Rambert dancers.

As ever, Ninette de Valois profited from Rambert's difficulties in keeping her company together. Many of the most valuable members of the Sadler's Wells Ballet had come from Rambert, Ashton, Turner, Chappell, Argyle. Now Peggy van Praagh left to join them as teacher, and eventually as director of the second company; two others, David Paltenghi a handsome actor/dancer and Pauline Clayden, one of Tudor's dancers, both joined de Valois; Walter Gore was called up into the navy, Frank Staff 'went commercial' as choreographer in the West End, presumably because he was South African he was not called up and was able to employ many of the Rambert dancers. Diana danced for a while until she married Yehudi Menuhin, Prudence Hyman was another who went 'commercial', it was inevitable that they wandered away, even if they were not financially destitute they realised that time was running out and they wanted to continue their careers.

The Ballet Rambert did not work as a troupe from September 1941 until March 1943, eighteen months, a long time in ballet terms, a long time physically for dancers already in their twenties, a time when the body begins to stiffen up, a time to turn around and look at life, a worrying time. The greatest loss was Maude Lloyd who gave up dancing when she married Nigel Gosling. She was thirty-one, not an age to hang around waiting for work; van Praagh was twenty-nine, not a good age to reshape a career although this is what she did, culminating in becoming director of the Australian Ballet. She particularly must have been bitterly disappointed at Tudor's 'defection' which is how his desertion of his company for the safety of America was viewed by the British. It would be many years before he was forgiven and invited back to choreograph for the Royal Ballet.

Those dancers who were left had no choice, they could not afford to hang around and Mim understood. There was something very special about that group of enthusiastic creators, to do with their emergence at that particular time in the thirties when new ground was being charted, their individual backgrounds, their idealism, the excitement of unexplored territory, in a way, their innocence. In today's media-oriented world, the plight of Mim and her company would have no doubt elicited attention from influential well-wishers, patrons of the arts and the press and something would have been done to keep this unique band of dancers and choreographers together – Rubin perhaps would have been bought out. But this was 1940.

While the Rambert company was going through all this drama, new ballet companies were forging ahead, touring the provinces, performing in the many Theatre Royals with their faithful clientele all over the British

Isles. The Empire or the Hippodrome staged variety and the other 'straight' theatres, built in the 1800s, presented the touring musicals, opera and ballet companies. Among those ballet companies were John Regan's Les Ballets Trois Arts, a gallant group of excellent dancers stranded in England because of the war (of which as Maria Sanina I was one) and who during the bitter winter of 1939/40 opened at the Lyric, Hammersmith. They gathered an enthusiastic audience of people who were prepared to trudge through the snow-laden unlit streets to capture a few hours of escapism. The bright, colourful Anglo-Polish Ballet opened with great success at the Apollo Theatre in Shaftesbury Avenue and subsequently played the best dates in the provinces, as did Mona Inglesby's International Ballet. And taking the lead were the Sadler's Wells company, gaining strength and recognition. It is ironic that the fountainhead that produced so much of the source material for all these companies was eventually, after release from bondage, relegated to touring factories and workers' clubs.

CEMA (The Council for the Encouragement of Music and the Arts) was the forerunner of the Arts Council. Along with ENSA it provided entertainment for the troops and the workers for the war effort. Although a wag nicknamed it The Council for the Encouragement of Mediocre Arts, CEMA did sterling work bringing the ballet to the masses and quite a few future dancers saw their first ballet performed in a works canteen. The little band of Rambert dancers, some very young, went everywhere, out of doors, inside factories, 'Workers' Playtime', and special hostels for the munitions workers. They had to put on their performance at times that accommodated the workers coming off or going on to their shift, sometimes at midnight.

They were accompanied by two pianists who must have suffered torture having to play on out-of-tune pianos. Small temporary stages, little more than platforms, adequate for singers and comedians but totally unsuitable for ballet, created problems especially for the girls' pointe-work in *Sylphides* when the male dancer wore Ashton's *Façade* trousers in place of white tights, as he certainly wasn't going to risk barracking from people who had never seen ballet in their life. Bobby Harrold, who received his baptism of fire on that tour remarked, 'We never got the bird or were even whistled at.' Sometimes they did a children's show 'and they fell about!'

There were no dressing-rooms so the boys had to change and make up in the gents' toilet, also a hazardous operation. They played in RAF camps, NAAFI canteens, only occasionally having the luxury of a real theatre. There was one fraught occasion when there was a double booking and the company had to be split in two. In normal circumstances the acute discomfort of such a tour would have been unacceptable but the constantly reiterated cry of 'Don't you know there's a war on?' was an excuse for a certain amount of slackness in organisation.

A lot of the venues were in secret locations, the dancers having no idea where they were, they travelled 'out into the wilds' in buses and trains. The factory workers wore their working get-up, the women in head scarves and overalls. I was also touring at the same period and I remember how shocked I was in Burnley on seeing the women with newspaper wrapped around their legs against the biting cold and hearing the ring of clogs over the cobblestones as they made their way to work. The dancers ate along with the workers in the canteens and having no coupons for anything better they dressed in the most ordinary clothes, besides, they did not want to attract attention to themselves. Nevertheless, they were regarded as some strange kind of species that had dropped in their midst, people were not unfriendly, just mystified as to how these cavorting elves had landed in their factory.

And what of Mim, that extraordinary woman steeped in snobbery? She went everywhere with her company and ate Spam and dried egg in the canteen, slept in the hostels along with the rest of them, almost relishing the experience. Perhaps she, who had shouted 'God Save The King' at her wedding, considered that she and the dancers were doing their bit for the war effort. Intensely patriotic toward her adopted country, she threw herself with enthusiasm into any situation. But although she was always there, Bobby said, 'We never knew what she really thought as she never discussed things with us and none of us really talked to her on friendly terms.' How sad, as she must have been very lonely, but she was never 'easy' company, you never felt completely relaxed with her. She had only to frown and purse her lips to stifle any advance in familiarity. But then her company were so much younger than herself, almost her grandchildren, and they came from such diverse backgrounds and were not always that interesting as people. She was interested in them as dancers and intended to keep them up to scratch, and together.

She had almost an obsession about training, to her the daily class was like Mass, a mantra, whatever the circumstances, whatever the conditions, her dancers had to go through their daily routine of the class. Aware perhaps that although she had talented young people they were not ideally suited to the exigencies of the classical technique she feared that given too much time off they would get lazy. Dancers who are naturally supple, apart from warming-up for a performance, can 'get away with murder', in other words born dancers, providing they do not let their technique slip, can make do without the grinding daily class. They will perform up to standard happily on tour and return to the daily class when they reach home base.

Rambert gave her classes in the most unlikely places, bidding them to hang on to whatever was available for the barre work, managing without a pianist, whistling shrilly as accompaniment. She would have them in the corridors of trains on a journey – in their day clothes doing their *battements tendus* hanging on to the window rail to the bewilderment of passengers trying to get to the toilet. They simply couldn't believe their eyes. On a memorable occasion when touring factories for CEMA they did class on the tarmac flat roof of a factory where they were to perform. It happened to be during a heat wave and as the lesson progressed the tar began to melt in the heat of the sun and the dancers ended up almost glued to the roof.

Bobby Harrold, after two deferments, was refused a third and was finally called up into the army. 'Being with Mim was an excellent preparation for army life, it was nearly a rest cure!'

CHAPTER 22

Although the post-war years took me away from the immediate orbit of the Rambert-Dukes family they were never far away, indeed, one way and another they seem to have been written into the story of my life.

In the 1940s my mother's business was flourishing and Mim was dividing her time between her school and her company. When she wasn't touring she would occasionally appear unanounced at 23 Yeoman's Row and settle herself in the armchair in my mother's workroom having peremptorily banished the cat, she didn't like animals. (On a visit to Lulu and her husband in the fifties when they were living in Trinidad, there was an uproar when Mim kicked their beloved dog, Don, Lu's husband, gave Mim such a dressing down that she wouldn't speak to him for the rest of the visit.)

Nursing a cup of tea on her lap she prattled away to my mother, the conversation inevitably turning to the subject of their children. Mim talked about her 'outlaws', in other words, the partners of their daughters. Angela was with David Ellis who eventually succeeded Rambert as director of Ballet Rambert. Ellis, although studying at Oxford to become a doctor, had also attended ballet classes before the war. Once he had qualified and moved to St George's Hospital in London, he had continued taking daily classes in Vera Volkova, the Russian teacher's, open classes in the West End where he met Angela.

Lulu's 'outlaw' was an ex-RAF pilot from St Vincent in the Caribbean. I had made a passionate but misguided liaison with a charismatic Polish ex-Merchant Navy man, handsome as Yul Brynner but without a penny to his name. My mother was bitterly disappointed that he had persuaded me to give up my ballet career for more lucrative work in the commercial theatre. Tony was the only one of us who had done things the proper way, now serving as an officer in the RAF he had married a very pretty girl who was the daughter of Mischa Spolianski, the composer. Eventually we all married, my marriage being the only one that did not endure.

Rambert greatly valued private life and was able to separate the professional woman in herself from the private person. She adored Ashley and suffered jealousy over his interest in other women and at one point in her marriage made a great effort to win him back. In truth she had 'let herself go', perhaps in reaction to her husband's continual absence and his loss of interest in her as a woman. Having abandoned her previous interest in fashion, the chic Parisienne had disappeared inside a selection of unremarkable garments, blouses, cardigans and skirts, sensible shoes, the typical middle-class Englishwoman's uniform. She always looked neat but although she had a perfect unlined skin and her eyes were as bright as ever, sensitive to her greying hair she dyed it a rather harsh black and scraped it back into a tight little bun.

In an attempt to win back Ashley she now took more trouble over her personal appearance, went for beauty treatments, regular visits to the hair dresser, bought some new clothes. She had phenomenally good health, ate very little, never touched alcohol and lived on fruit and yoghourt. This was hardly a companion for Ashley whose girth had expanded considerably over the years and who loved his drink, his food and pretty women. The estrangement from her husband remained. When in old age Rambert allowed her hair to go white, had it cut short and permed, the transformation was most attractive, as Snowdon's portraits of her in the eighties demonstrate.

The fortunes of Ballet Rambert went up and down like the temperature graph of an ailing patient. In 1945 they toured Germany for three months, this time for ENSA. Ashley was working as cultural advisor for music and drama with the Control Commission in Berlin. In her memoir Mim wrote proudly of the good work he was doing. He stayed there for two years which no doubt gave him satisfaction but his absence from taking any active part in the doings of the Mercury and particularly of Ballet Rambert contributed to the financial crisis that ensued during those two years.

After the ENSA tour in 1946 the company had reformed itself preparatory to its first season at Sadler's Wells, an event which became a yearly tradition. Many dancers returned and bright new ones graduated from the school; there was a new feeling of exhilaration and enthusiasm at what was virtually a rebirth. CEMA had evolved into the Arts Council and sponsored the season, refurbishing a full-length production of *Giselle* that won the universal acclaim of the most eminent dance critics and the public, triumphantly reinstating the reputation of Ballet Rambert.

It is interesting to ponder Rambert's love and understanding of this ballet. There were so many contradictions in her nature, for in spite of her apparent appetite for the avant garde, was she really true to herself, one wonders? Or was she too easily influenced by fashion? She was at heart a woman who belonged to the romantic age of Théophile Gautier, and had a great love of pure classicism. In her book she wrote how 'she was moved at each performance' of her *Giselle* and almost as an afterthought adds, 'It had the same effect on the audience'. This was her strength and her weakness, her own delight and pride in her dancers and ballets often blinded her to faults that a more ruthlessly professional eye such as de Valois, would have noticed. But in the case of *Giselle* performed by a strong cast headed by Sally Gilmour, Walter Gore and Joyce Graeme, her pride was quite justified. The dancers were happy with renewed faith in the future.

But in spite of having re-established itself as a major company at the Wells the fortunes of the company fluctuated alarmingly. In 1946 there was a tour of Scotland where the company had to split in half in order to be able to visit different venues. Although nowadays this often happens with a large company Rambert was the first in this field, but it diluted the strength and enthusiasm of the long-suffering dancers who found the touring hard and uncomfortable.

Money was the perennial problem, the Arts Council support for the company was sporadic and they suffered the eternal drawback of being under-funded. Rambert was no business-woman and certainly not extravagant in her expenditure on costumes and décor, quite the opposite, but without a guaranteed sum far in excess of the grant from the Council she simply could not make ends meet. Forced to lose their treasured independence, Mim and Ashley were using their own money but by the summer of 1947 when another twelve-week season at the Wells was planned, the financial situation had become very serious indeed.

Ashley, still in Berlin, tried to rescue the situation. He wrote to the Council that Mim 'had already lost more than she received in salary and rental for the ballet in the past two years', and asked for an advance on the twice-yearly grant to 'Save the situation and tide her over'.

The second Wells season turned out a disaster. 'My blackest hour', Mim declared. There was a heatwave, the theatres were empty, in any case by today's standards twelve weeks was far too long. The orchestra of inferior quality which had toured with them was expensive and had to be laid off for the last few weeks when the Musicians' Union made trouble. The company returned to two pianos, an ignominious climb-down even though the pianists were of the best.

Given the variety of the existing repertoire which included *Plaisance*, a charming ballet by Walter Gore, it might be thought that the launching of yet more ballets was an unnecessary burden. However, there is a long tradition of new ballets for a London season in the ballet world and Mim's voracious appetite for new choreography was her *cause célèbre*.

Andrée came up with *The Sailor's Return* to a score by Arthur Oldham and based on David Garnett's novel. When it transpired that there was not enough money to hire people to create costumes and scenery, Andrée returned to the typical old Ballet Club tradition of do-it-yourself. Andrée, brilliantly gifted woman that she was, set to with scissors and paint, designed and made the costumes herself and even painted the décor. She had great difficulty in extracting her cast out of Rambert's frenetic rehearsals for fittings and there were altercations between Mim and herself which culminated in Mim offering to stand in for the dancers. However she soon got fed up with the boring business of standing being pinned into a costume. Finally a truce was declared and the cast released for their fittings. My mother over the years made many costumes for Andrée including *La Fête Ètrange* but although she greatly admired Andrée she dreaded her visits to the workroom. Having always made her own clothes she was critical and pernickety and so hard to please that my mother often wondered why Andrée asked her to make anything at all.

The Sailor's Return was a great success but could not salvage a disastrous season and since there was no piano score the ballet was ditched once the orchestra had departed, perhaps 'sunk' would be a more apt metaphor. Despondency descended on Rambert and her company who, in spite of poor houses, had enjoyed the season. So much endeavour, so much enthusiasm and at the end, nothing. Yet once again they were back on the tiny Mercury stage, but some of the dancers like Elisabeth Schooling who had stayed on through so many ups and downs could not face it any more and left.

And then the miracle happened, as it sometimes does in the theatre. A six-month contract for a tour of Australia based, according to Rambert, on a visit to a particularly bad matinee by an impresario called Dan O'Connor who, despite the empty house, declared 'the company had danced as though at a great Gala!' which so enchanted Mim that she accepted his offer immediately.

By now Mim and Ashley were heavily in debt. On the basis of this contract Ashley asked for an advance from the Arts Council on the undertaking that the loan would be repaid out of the proceeds from the Australian tour. Ashley pleaded with the Council to 'advise Mme Rambert in her extreme difficulty'. He even suggested that 'For instance, she can raise a fairly large sum from the sale of her ballet print collection which I formed for her and intended eventually to offer to one of the museums on her behalf.' (For the record the collection did go eventually to the Victoria & Albert Museum. The prints were dumped in the basement out of the public eye for many years until they finally ended up in the Theatre Museum.)

Mim and Ashley now had no alternative but to 'hold out the begging bowl' which Mim so hated. Ashley asked a patron of the company if 'Mme Rambert can be put in the way of finding some lender who will produce the necessary funds secured as loan on the Australian contract and the properties of the ballet'. He adds, 'Our immediate difficulty arises more from bad luck than mismanagement or misdirection.' This from the arrogant Ashley Dukes shows a man in extremity. The begging letters went out to people who had been admirers of the Ballet Club, including Cyril Beaumont who sent them a loan of one hundred pounds and wrote, 'I do hope you will soon be able to dispose of your immediate worries and that the wheel of fortune will turn once more in your favour and remain there.'

Mim was thoroughly upset by the constant financial crisis and there were rows that reverberated around the walls of the Mercury. At one point she declared that she would terminate her present company and and start anew with dancers from the school, a threat not taken seriously by her husband who merely dismissed it as 'Mim having one of her turns'.

Eventually Ballet Rambert did go off to Australia and New Zealand and, although not all of her dancers agreed to go, they set off in September 1947 with a strong cast and refurbished costumes and scenery.

Australia had an appetite for ballet developed over several years of various tours. First the Anna Pavlova tours, the visits of the Ballets Russes in 1937, 1938 and 1939 and then the continuation of that tradition with the efforts of the Russian émigrés, especially Borovansky, who remained behind in 1939 and founded the predecessor of the Australian Ballet company.

The Rambert company, however, was something quite different and it took the Australian audiences some time to accustom themselves to the unusual repertoire. It is interesting that the name of Rambert today represents modern ballet, and even the Australians when they were first confronted with ballets in a style quite different from the Russian repertoire were taken aback, by the Tudor works particularly. They concluded that this was modern ballet and this was before the radical change when the company jettisoned almost the entire repertory that had been presented in the Antipodes.

Apart from the few splashes of success such as the first Wells season Mim was not really appreciated in England and did not get the recognition she deserved until many years later. The Australians boosted her confidence, perhaps they understood the character of her company and

Mim herself, who after all was one more foreigner in a country into which more and more foreigners were taking refuge. Hostesses vied with each other to entertain this unusual band of dancers who valued interpretative dance more highly than great technical feats of athleticism. Mim was invited to give talks to organisations all over the country. She spoke with no notes, and with such passion, such eloquence that she mesmerised and enchanted the culture-hungry matrons and their long-suffering husbands. Mim was of course a born showman and she was able to indulge in her own favourite role of being the star performer of her company.

She always gave a curtain speech at the end of each season, standing in the midst of her company, the stage strewn with bouquets, performing her *grande révérence* and coming forward to give her farewell speech in the most gracious manner of the grande dame and then astounding her audience by turning a cartwheel! It was outrageous, but she got away with it. The company looked on like indulgent parents smiling, some of them ironically.

A tour which had been booked for six months was extended to sixty-seven weeks. During that period some dancers returned to England, some Australians joined up to replace them. Some made the decision to settle in Australia. When in 1949 the Ballet Rambert set sail for England, it was reported that out of 26 dancers only 12 returned.

CHAPTER 23

Angela and David did not go on the Australian tour. Now married, they decided to take up an offer from the government of Colombia to found a national ballet school and company. Unfortunately their work was disrupted by the outbreak of civil war and they were repatriated after twelve months, returning in 1950. Angela returned to teaching at the Mercury and David began to make plans to fill the vacuum left by the absence of Ballet Rambert.

David had gained valuable experience during the war years when he took part in a variety of productions , working with opera companies and Molly Lake's Embassy Ballet, and on films and arranging two evenings for television with Philip Bates, staging *Jardin aux lilas*. In 1951, he and Angela founded Ballet Workshop, a project for the presentation of new and experimental productions by aspiring choreographers in the hopes of discovering a new generation of choreographers for Ballet Rambert, much needed at that period in the company's fortunes.

A most important element was the encouragement of new composers and new designers. Inevitably some of the ballets were less successful than others but since in the old Ballet Club tradition the performances were on Sunday nights the workshop was able to recruit good dancers despite their other professional commitments. Rehearsals had to be snatched to fit into the professional schedules of the participants who gave their services free.

The performances attracted packed audiences and the atmosphere recalled the days of the Ballet Club. It also attracted many established choreographers; Jack Carter, Walter Gore and Michael Holmes all presented new works that were almost all transferred to other companies. But the quality of most of the ballets with one or two exceptions did not compare to those of the past. The post-war generation of would-be choreographers did not have the innocence and excitement of discovery of the thirties. They were a different breed, already a little blasé, they had worked in the theatre during the forties, either in touring ballet companies or the musicals and revues that proliferated during that period, and there seemed to be a lack of imagination, or inspiration in many of the works presented on that historic stage. Some were amateurish and only saved by the quality of the music and décor, but this was to be expected from an experimental enterprise.

The perennial problem with choreography is that apart from a brief outline, there is no equivalent of a script that can be assessed before the project is undertaken. Steps and moves, development of the theme, musicality, drama, all of this can only evolve in the rehearsal room 'live' as it were and the whole picture can only be perceived when the work is finished and it is too late to withdraw should it not succeed. David and Angela were good directors and proved they could run a theatrical enterprise with skill and efficiency.

I took part in two of the productions in 1952 and 1954, *Movimientos*, an interesting piece by Michael Charnley, and *The Life and Death of Lola Montez* by Jack Carter. Charnley had trained at Dartington Hall under Kurt Jooss and had been a member of the Ballet Jooss. Extremely gifted, he brought a fresh approach to choreography evolving a fund of original and – in those days – very modern movement. Whereas the Jooss dancers had shortcomings in their lack of classical ballet training Charnley had a firm grasp of both styles and was able to mould them into a whole. But for his mercurial and unpredictable temperament he should have made his mark on British Ballet alongside Walter Gore and later Christopher Bruce. His *Movimientos* to specially written music by Michael Hobson attracted the attention of Julian Braunsweg, then director of London Festival Ballet, and Anton Dolin who came to the performance. Charnley was engaged to mount a ballet to Don Gillis's *Symphony for Fun*. Braunsweg proudly wrote that it was Festival Ballet's first contemporary work. The ballet was a great success and it was hoped that Charnley would develop into a major choreographer. In 1953 he mounted *Alice in Wonderland* for Festival Ballet which was very popular and in some ways pre-empted Ashton's *Tales of Beatrix Potter*. Perhaps he was a little too lightweight for a ballet company and was lured to the West End, where he earned large fees choreographing for revue. This really proved his downfall, as apart from a work for Festival Ballet in 1956, *Homage to a Princess*, he continued his work in the West End. Unfortunately the ballet profession considered him difficult and too commercial and dropped him. Tragically he became an alcoholic and died quite young in poverty and obscurity.

In 1951 Ashley Dukes was very much around, an overpowering presence hovering in the hallway eyeing the dancers with distaste as we crept past him into his precious theatre. He had not changed over the years and still regarded Mim's 'schoolchildren' with suspicion, with some justification it has to be said. From time to time he would appear through the doors of the auditorium to chastise us for some misdemeanour such as sitting on top of the upright piano parked next to the stage, or munching

sandwiches in the stalls or, in the manner of all weary dancers, slumping in the tip-up seats with our legs thrown over the back of the row in front of us.

Charnley and I were appearing at the Players' Theatre during the week and rehearsed a lively pas de deux to Strauss's *Tritsch Tratsch Polka* that I had danced in the Anglo-Polish ballet. Michael and I couldn't afford to hire a studio so we rehearsed in secret on the Mercury stage in the lunch hour. I was the can-can dancer 'à la Danilova' to Charnley's moustachioed waiter balancing a tray on his hand in the fashion of Léonide Massine in *Gaîeté Parisienne*. We were doing a kind of juggling act as officially Michael was choreographing a solo for me for *Movimientos*. We rehearsed *Tritsch-Tratsch* to an old-fashioned wind-up gramophone concealed in the wings stopping in mid step the moment there was a sighting of the ominous Ashley through the doors and hastily returning to my very intense solo. We'd taken the precaution of placing a friend in a strategic position to warn us.

The company returned from Australia bankrupt. Ashley had been worried for some time at the lack of communication and deficiencies in the accounting but at such a distance there was nothing he could do. It transpired that the manager, Dan O'Connor, had disappeared taking all the money and somewhere along the line lost the costumes and scenery. It seems incredible that such a thing could happen to such a prestigious ballet company in the fifties. Such negligence of business seems extraordinary, but there it was.

The Ellises were still running Ballet Workshop; the company or what remained of it after the Australian debacle, was being run by David Paltenghi. Mim herself at this time seemed rather grim, no wonder, as she had no part in Ballet Workshop and there was none of that former ebullience. She seemed a lonely figure, distrait, her marriage no consolation, her daughters taken up with husbands and children. She was abandoned by many of her dancers who either stayed in Australia or left in disgust at the realisation that there was no work for them in England. Nothing had been arranged except a return to that tiny little stage once more.

'It was too much', Elisabeth Schooling said, 'I just couldn't stand it any more', and she left, this time for good. 'After sticking to Mim throughout the war doing awful dates, the company expected a London season, but we found ourselves back at the Mercury. She had no confidence in her company, no push, never could expand, she was afraid to leave that building which seemed safe, she simply would not take a chance.' But then dancers in those days never understood the complexities of running ballet companies and indeed were not encouraged to understand.

Schooling was disappointed that Ninette de Valois never invited her and Sally into the Sadler's Wells company. Frank Staff who could have been a great asset to de Valois at that time was not invited because according to Schooling, 'he blotted his copy book'. How, Liz never explained, Frank was an outspoken South African not accustomed to the subtleties of the English and was probably rude to de Valois.

And here was Mim, an elderly, colourless little figure, not exactly ignored but somehow brushed aside by a new generation of young people busy with their own ambitions. She was learning the bitter lesson that to be missing is to be forgotten. The company went on a tour of Scotland in the bitter cold doing one-night stands, the most arduous and taxing form of touring. The fifties was to be a hard, dispiriting period when once again Ballet Rambert faced extinction.

Bored with this period of relative inactivity, Mim frequently visited married members of her old company, which to them was almost a Royal visitation. Although Mim herself disliked sycophancy she was nonetheless careful to pick the best houses. Like Queen Elizabeth I she had the habit of deciding to stay with people without warning and would simply announce her intention to stay, literally forcing herself on people. 'We didn't have two pennies to rub together', John Andrewes reminisced, 'but our financial difficulties never seemed to occur to her'.

When Schooling remarried she and her husband Michael Chaplin went to farm in Devon, not altogether Elisabeth's choice, but the house and its location were delightful. A barn was converted into a studio and Elisabeth acquired some promising pupils, a few of whom were assimilated into the Royal Ballet School and the Rambert School. Mim would visit the Chaplins quite often, behaving with her usual eccentricity and putting quite a strain on the household. They were surprised when after breakfast she announced that she was 'going out for a roll'. 'I think she means a stroll', Elisabeth mused. Mim asked a surprised Michael to lend her his raincoat. Several sizes too big for her, she wrapped herself up in it, marched out into the garden and seeing a steep slope, lay down and rolled all the way down to the bottom. Scrambling to her feet and shaking herself like a terrier she assured her amused hosts that this was wonderful for the circulation. This performance took place every morning during her stay.

Elisabeth was an excellent cook and went to great pains to produce tasty meals for Rambert. After Mim had departed they received a letter thanking them for their hospitality but adding a footnote to the effect that the food had not agreed with her and Helen, her housekeeper, had had to give her an aperient to settle her digestion. Elisabeth was furious.

My brief return to the Mercury to perform in Ballet Workshop did nothing to kindle any nostalgia in me. Having danced on big stages I found the lack of space on the stage and the closeness of the audience almost embarrassing and was rather hurt that Rambert herself paid scant attention to me. She probably regarded me as a deserter and she was unforgiving. It is therefore all the more surprising that eventually, in the late fifties, when I had made a thorough mess of both my career and my personal life that it was she, through Angela, who threw me a lifeline and drew me back into the fold. But it took some time for the prodigal to be forgiven.

The 1950s found me earning my living working in films, revues, musicals and a six-month spell at the little Players Theatre 'underneath the arches' in Charing Cross. The last time I danced on stage was in *The King and I* at the Theatre Royal in Drury Lane in 1953. I had damaged my back quite seriously from neglect over the years and once *The King and I* completed the two-and-a-half years run, I became ill and underwent a major gynaecological operation which left me weak and debilitated.These were disillusioning years when I bitterly regretted having virtually abandoned the ballet world, but I was at a bit of a crossroads in my private life.

I kept in practice at the West Street Studio where Anna Northcote and Vera Volkova held open classes for professionals. There, friends would meet up and after class trot along to Chez Valérie in Soho for coffee and a good gossip. However, although almost every dancer living and working in London turned up at some time or other, including Margot Fonteyn, I never recall meeting a Rambert dancer. Their home base was the Mercury towards which they migrated, taking Mim's classes and endlessly rehearsing, sometimes for only two performances. Having returned from a triumphantly successful tour of Australia only to find themselves without any future engagements they were a dispirited group, out of work for a lot of that year. Although quite a few of the dancers had elected to stay in Australia, others clung loyally to Rambert waiting for better times. Had they not had that base in Notting Hill Gate it is doubtful whether Ballet Rambert would have continued to exist. Rambert who herself was known to sulk for three days at a time, would not tolerate this from her dancers, in her opinion the cure for depression was to work harder and she had no time for emotional indulgence. It was this very spirit that kept her dancers going.

Lulu and I were good friends and we used to meet from time to time, when I heard news about Rambert and the company. Ballet Workshop had taken me back briefly to the Mercury stage in early 1951 but that was to be my only contact for some time. There was little work for the vastly depleted company until June when they went on an arduous tour of remote areas of Scotland. It smacked of their wartime touring days for ENSA. Glancing through the list of engagements for the early fifties there is a heterogeneous collection of performances ranging from a week in Butlins holiday camp in Skegness to a rather bizarre pairing of the first act of *Giselle* with Rossellini's production of *St Joan at the Stake* starring Ingrid Bergman at the Stoll Theatre. Several plans including one for a visit to the United States came to nothing. Some performances were for only two nights, such as at Aix-les-Bains. These disparate bookings were a means of keeping the group together although some of the best dancers left. In 1953 Sally Gilmour gave a farewell performance at the Lyric prior to leaving for Australia with her new husband. She was a great loss to Mim and adored by the company. She embodied the style and philosophy of the Rambert dancer.

In 1951 I was approached by Leonard Sachs, the former chairman of the Players' Theatre, to form a small ensemble and choreograph for his project for the Festival of Britain. Lulu joined me along with Anne Wakefield as one of 'Mr Sach's Sylphides' in the pretty little bandbox of a theatre designed by Guy Shepherd in Battersea pleasure gardens. Leonard, a delightful ebullient man, planned to found another Victorian music hall venue featuring most of the original artists from the Players. Since many of the artists could only appear after their West End work the show started at 10pm. This was way past the bedtime of the average promenader of the park, particularly in the appalling wet weather of that year. Battersea was off limits for a West End audience, especially on a dark, muddy night. The result was empty houses.

Interestingly, down the road Andrée Howard was arranging a ballet version of *Orlando the Marmalade Cat* to launch the newly built open-air Theatre in the Park. The cast was almost entirely Rambert, the dancers thankful to have a reasonably well-paid job to fill in until the next tour. Although the ballet was quite entertaining Andrée's rather special qualities were not suitable for a drop-in audience who understood it no more than they understood our own 'Mr Sach's Song Saloon'. While the dancers kept dry under the shelter of the stage canopy the meagre scattering of public were soaked to the skin. It was a dismal experience for all of us and a total flop from the point of view of the organisers of the Festival. Although the

Marmalade Cat was supposed to be a ballet for children it could not compete with the funfair crowded with raucous children whooping with delight on the big dipper.

It was Lulu who having worked with me during that time told me I would make a good teacher. 'You have such patience', she said. It was some time later that I received a phone call from Angela inviting me to teach at the Mercury.

CHAPTER 24

I returned to teach at the Mercury in 1959. I was 38, and had been almost invalided out of my profession by a back injury. My mother had died after a long fight with cancer in 1955 and my marriage had ended in divorce. I was at a loss as to what to do with my life and reluctant to take up an occupation that I had always thought rather thankless. Lulu, who had taught there for several years, was escaping the unsympathetic English climate which her husband, reared in St Vincent in the Caribbean, found unbearable. With their two children they emigrated to Trinidad where Lu founded a ballet school. She was never to return to England, for Rambert a great sadness.

I had been working in the cheerful, democratic world of the commercial theatre and at first found the cloistered atmosphere at the Mercury as precious and constraining as ever. However, I found comfort in the realisation that I would be under the same roof as Ballet Rambert and hoped in due course to be somehow associated with them. Although the company rarely rehearsed at the Mercury the management occupied the front office and the school used the former greenroom as an office. One would have thought that this arrangement would have kept alive the liaison between school and company, but I was to be disappointed in this as in a few years there would be a schism that resulted in the Ballet Rambert moving out and almost severing ties with the school.

After Ashley Dukes died in 1959 there were renewed efforts to build a theatre in his memory. To quote David Ellis, 'Ashley had originally planned for Elidir Davies to build the theatre, it was he who built the Mermaid Theatre in the City, but he withdrew after getting involved in a scandal in the Caribbean. Then out of the blue, Colonel Seerest (who built Centrepoint) sent his designs, unsolicited, to the papers, which created chaos.'

Eventually a design by Basil Spence was chosen. Peter Hall, who was looking for a permanent home for the Royal Shakespeare, came up with the proposal that the theatre should be shared between the two companies, divided into three seasons, one for Rambert, one for the Shakespeare and the third season kept open for visiting companies. It seemed the perfect solution and plans went ahead to make an announcement to the press. A vast international dinner was arranged at Hampton Court Palace to launch the plan. A huge model of the projected theatre was displayed to the excitement and plaudits of the delighted audience, when suddenly the evening developed into a farce. *The Evening Standard* had announced that Peter Hall had pulled out at the eleventh hour having come to an agreement to go to the Barbican. Everyone went home. This story seems to encapsulate the list of perpetual failures that seemed to dog Ballet Rambert. The theatre site was eventually sold after Rambert's death in 1982. Ashley's dream was never fulfilled. Jane Pritchard wrote, 'It was only then that the company's long dream of their own dance house finally faded.'

It was a strange experience to return after twenty-three years to a building that had scarcely changed. It brought back memories of my mother and Tony and myself, as a hard-working, anxious young girl eager to go out into the exciting world of a ballet company and leave behind those long arduous years of training. Now I was an experienced professional, buffeted and bruised by life, estranged from the ballet profession by my incursions into the commercial world of theatre. But I had to admit to myself that there was a feeling of coming home, something to do with the smell of the place, of familiarity, that same passage, with the same paint work, even the lino had not been renewed, the same double doors leading into what was once the little theatre, now a studio but with the tiny stage intact. Rambert, now seventy, still taught when she was not with the company, and was still the titular director. But the school was run by Angela, now an experienced teacher, David Ellis being director of the company, which added to Angela's status.

The other prominent personality was that extraordinary woman Erica Bowen, whom I did not know. An effusive middle-aged woman in too tight clothes and a Veronica Lake hairdo, Erica acted as Rambert's secretary along with her other many roles. John Drummond happened to be lodging with Erica at that time and in his book *Tainted by Experience*, described her as 'a capricious creature who on some days would insist you joined her for dinner, on others make it only too clear that you were not wanted. On New Year's Eve she decided to re-upholster a chair and abandon any attempt at celebration.' She celebrated my first day as teacher at the school by taking me back to her flat for a drink and making me drunker than I had ever been in my life on vast quantities of gin and vermouth.

During Mim's long absence in Australia, Angela and her husband being away at that time teaching in Bogotá, the school had been run by Erica which rather turned her head and was a constant source of irritation to Angela. She was a capable and resourceful woman who worshipped Mim with the kind of passion Rambert inspired in her admirers. Mrs Bowen was a character, an oddity who might have found difficulty in obtaining a job in a more conventional establishment, but admirably fitted the eccentricities of the Rambert School. Secretary, nurse, counsellor, caterer, cook, procurer of second-hand refurbishment and general mopper-upper, she slaved away for glory, underpaid and overworked. In fact she knew very little about ballet, one suspects did not even particularly like it, but it was the intellectual side of Mim's personality and the kudos attached to the job that attracted her.

Although the school was now run on a sound financial basis, thanks to the introduction of student grants, nothing had changed where the teachers were concerned. 'Honour and glory' was still the ethos that prevailed from the early days of Mim and Ashley. You were not expected to actually *need* money, that had to be got from elsewhere and it was assumed that you had private means. Many of the teachers of that period did indeed have private means, it sometimes seemed to me that in that respect also nothing had changed. I still did not have any money! We were paid so much an hour and there was no pay for holidays, and no pensions.

The school was well run on a tight budget. Reared in a hard school herself, Angela was a strong personality, like her mother in many ways but lacking Mim's charm. Having in her youth endured the lacerations of her mother's cruel tongue and the hurly-burly of life in the itinerant Rambert company, she understood the needs of the students far better than she was sometimes given credit for. The dilettante daughters of rich families belonged to the past, now the grant system ensured that professional training was available to talented young people from every walk of life.

We had no illusions about the need for the students to find employment at the end of their training. To this end we worked tirelessly in our efforts to guide and promote them. We established a connection with German opera houses where English dancers were welcomed and at graduation packed them off to audition armed with instructions on their appearance, train times, addresses of digs, how to address the Ballet Master and numerous other admonitions, advice that ensured they returned scathed but triumphantly waving a contract.

During my absence the school had acquired an extension in the shape of an Educational School, started by David Ellis and one of the first to incorporate formal education with ballet training for promising children from the age of ten. These were the pride and joy of Mim and Angela, among them Christopher Bruce who would one day become the company's director. The row of shops opposite above which the Kelly family had once lived were now the Educational School, although you would never have guessed it by the dilapidated and unchanged exterior of the building. The inside wasn't much better either, the Dickensian rooms crumbling with neglect.

The general decrepitude of the premises was not reflected in the activities within it. The department was run in association with the tutorial college Davies's Tutors who supplied the teachers. The headmistress, Margaret Cockburn (BA Oxon.), was the wife of a judge and a great ballet lover. A tall, stately woman of immense charm and culture, she was adored by pupils and teachers alike. The education was carried up to G.C.E standard. The fees were £58 per 14-week term for education and ballet training. The upper school was 5 guineas for 12 lessons. When Robin Howard became involved with helping to save the school in the late 1970s he was incredulous to discover that the fees for training at this prestigious school were the lowest in London for ballet training, but money had never been paramount in the minds of its founders.

The curriculum included singing, musical appreciation, art, regular visits to art galleries and museums, and G.C.E in music. Josephine Turnbull, who joined when she was 14, recalled, 'We had everything a scholar needed, teachers, morning milk and biscuits, lunch, loos, desks and chairs, blackboards, and all the basic subjects. The fact that the staircase shook gently if taken "on the run" or that the loos had no windows was of no consequence. It was none too warm in winter and the open electric fires dotted around the schoolrooms would have given today's Health and Safety regulators a nervous breakdown!'

Erica organised the lunches for the schoolchildren which took place in the basement studio directly after the class finished at 12.30. The moment the students vacated the still steaming studio the boys, dripping with sweat from their arduous class with Mim or Angela, would move in and erect four rickety trestle tables (obtained cheap by Erica), lay out the secondhand cutlery and place a bowl of oranges in the middle, one for each child. Erica in the wretched little scullery of the original house, none too clean and badly in need of a coat of paint, brewed up a cauldron of some mysterious stew which had been prepared at home in her own flat. Vegetables, already prepared by the boys were cooked on top of the elderly gas stove.

At 12.45 the children tumbled into the street to cross a main road to reach the Mercury on the other side, up the steps, through the hall, down the steep narrow basement stairs, crowded into the studio, all forty of them, and seated themselves at the tables. The meal was served by the boys at the end of which, bang on 1.30, they cleared everything away, marshalled by the commanding Erica. Each child, armed with their own rug, lay down on the floor, the doors were closed and while Erica and her helpers washed up in the inadequate old sink the children had a half-hour's nap. 'What a bore that was', recalled Jo, they were supposed to cover themselves with the rug, but after the boys and girls were discovered 'canoodling' under the blanket Erica changed the rules and the blankets were spread out and they rested for half-an-hour. At 2 o'clock sharp they gathered themselves up, dusted themselves down and marched out and back to school. At 2.30 the afternoon students filed into the room ready for their Cecchetti class.

As senior teacher I was given the special privilege of a dressing-room to myself, a half room actually. Originally one back room, when the thirties conversion took place this was divided in two, one part for Ashley Dukes's former office, little more than a passage where I changed, rested and listened to the confidences of tearful or rebellious students. The other half of this room had been transformed into the gentlemen's lavatory. Although the partitioning appeared solid enough the gentle sound of urination followed by the pull of the chain and the sound of cascading water provided a gentle obligato to my efforts at a quick snooze on the three-legged chaise-longue propped up by an unreliable block of wood. There was a small, ancient gas-fire that during the cold winters hissed and popped but gave off no appreciable heat since half the elements were broken. It gave off a gentle odour which probably aided me in my efforts to relax but had I remained there for too long would certainly have exterminated me or at best sent me into a coma. The floor of this spartan room was covered by a threadbare piece of carpet, another treasure Erica had picked up from her rag-and-bone woman and was thick with the dust of ages.

I appreciated the few pictures on the walls; good quality engravings of Mrs Siddons as Lady Macbeth elaborately dressed in eighteenth-century costume, and another of David Garrick in breeches, curly wig and elaborate coat declaiming Shakespeare. The only other lithograph depicted an elegant eighteenth-century ballet master, wearing a black velvet suit, white stockings, powdered wig, feet well turned out and wielding a baton. Perpetually bundled up in black wool against the damp and cold, I envied this sprightly gentleman who doubtless was regarded with respect by students and courtiers alike as the third highest paid member of the entourage of the Sun King at Versailles. I reflected grimly that things had not changed for the better in the 1960s.

Along the wall of my sanctuary was a long shelf crammed with bound albums of *Theatre Arts Monthly*, the publication for which Ashley Dukes had contributed articles so many years ago. The shabbiness of the vault-like room together with these engravings and books emphasised the scorn for material comforts of the owners and reminded me that material things were replaceable, great art was not. I warmed to David Garrick who looked out directly at me from his frame and often confided to him my difficulties in coming to terms with the painful realisation that my performing days were over.

The Ellises and their two children lived upstairs, 'above the shop'. The staircase in the old house was just above my dressing-room and the sound of Angela crashing down and slamming the door behind her reverberates in my memory of Friday evenings. The end of the working week left me after my last class drained of energy, longing for my home and a good drink. In would charge Angela, refreshed after an afternoon off, to have what she called 'a good natter'. This invariably consisted of complaints about her mother. For a good twenty minutes she railed against Mim and the hurtful things she had said, her misdemeanours, Angela unloading her own frustrations while I vainly tried to pacify her. It was no good, those two women were totally incompatible and continually rubbed each other up the wrong way. Angela was getting on for sixty and Mim well into her eighties, but it made no difference, old grudges were brought up. I was too tired to take in what this was all about but Angela could not get over her memories of her unhappy childhood. By the time she left the room and happily charged back upstairs I was a nervous wreck.

When I retired from the Mercury Angela asked me which engraving I would prefer as a leaving present. The alternative to Garrick was a lithograph of Taglioni that hung in the office. For a moment I hesitated, I had grown fond of Garrick but loyalty to my occupation won the day and I chose Taglioni.

When I returned to teach at the Mercury the policy of the upper school had not changed and still took on adult male 'starters' sometimes aged over twenty. Neither had Mim's training methods changed over the years and she dispensed the same treatment to gentle Jimmy Palmer as she had to Hugh Laing all those years ago. Jimmy recalls her standing facing him at the barre and giving directions while he worked:

'Pull in your stomach! Pull down your shoulders! Straighten your knees! Hold up your head! Lengthen your neck', she ordered.

'By then I was totally paralysed', Jimmy said. 'At the end of the barre-work we had to shoulder the leg, can-can fashion, then crash down onto the floor in a split, agony for the men and if your foot wasn't pointed she'd stand on it!'

But she made them laugh when with an impish glint in her eye she would start showing off, like the occasion when she lifted her skirt and, pretending to hold a cigar in her other hand, slunk round the studio doing the tango from *A Tragedy of Fashion*.

However, there were rumblings of discontent, particularly among the men, more outspoken than the girls although by the 1960s dancers had found their voice. They chafed under the overlong barre work, at the heavy adages and too-complicated enchainements and while they were amused by her personality they did not always appreciate her old-fashioned jokes. These boys and girls on government grants from all over the country did not understand Mim's wit, which could be interpreted as sarcasm.

The Educational School was another failure in the list of failures that seemed to track the fate of the Mercury. It was closed down in 1969. A letter written to the parents explained: 'The main reason for closure being that when it was opened it was thought that our new theatre, incorporating a completely rebuilt school would be ready in a few years. However, owing to the economic situation it has been found impossible to carry out this plan.' An unsubsidised private ballet school is very difficult to maintain, David had visualised an integrated school and company housed in their own projected theatre, but his plan had to be abandoned and the older pupils were assimilated into the upper school. Some of the younger ones were accepted by White Lodge, the Royal Ballet's lower school, by then established, or else they went to other professional schools.

A bonus of returning to the Mercury as a mature person was the opportunity to get to know Rambert, inasmuch as anybody could get to know this complex character. In addition to the day-to-day contact of teaching I was often invited to accompany her to performances as a kind of lady-in-waiting, a role I enjoyed far more than Angela, who refused to accompany her mother since it made her feel like 'Princess Margaret accompanying the Queen'. For me, untrammelled by a close relationship, it was an honour and besides, I could never have afforded to sit in the front stalls of the Opera House.

Accompanying Rambert was tantamount to keeping up with a whirlwind. Although now in her seventies she could still move through a crowd with a speed and ruthlessness that scattered all around her and without a backward glance. Her progress through the stage door could be embarrassing if by any ill-luck the doorman did not know who she was. We often conversed in French which gave us both great pleasure and afforded an extra link in companionship. Sometimes she would utter in a loud stage whisper an amusing but tactless remark on the merits of an unfortunate performer which would reduce me to a fit of giggles which naturally enough was accompanied by loud shushes from irate neighbours who hopefully did not understand French.

On one memorable occasion I accompanied her to a performance by Zizi Jeanmaire and her husband Roland Petit, both great friends of Mim. Our house seats were in the fourth row of the stalls and the overture played by Michel Le Grand and his band was deafening. After two or three minutes being blasted out of our seats Mim sprang to her feet, rushed up to the orchestra rail and shouted 'Shut up!' and then ran to the back of the auditorium where she remained for the rest of the show. The people sitting near us were vastly amused and probably sympathised with her. I stayed in my seat until the interval when I skulked backstage after her where she let out a tirade to Petit about his famous orchestra.

But then there were the golden moments when she was at her best and even after so many years could inspire me as no other mentor had. There was the time I escorted her to a lecture she was giving to the Friends of Covent Garden in her early eighties. I had recently passed my driving test and she had told me that I might drive her to the theatre as she trusted me. She insisted on sitting in the back and if for a moment I turned my head to address her she commanded 'No, no Breegy, don't turn your head, look where you are going.'

I sat in the stalls of a dark and empty Opera House one cold Sunday evening among a group of elderly ladies, Friends of Covent Garden. The Opera House looked strangely unlike its glamorous self on this cold Sunday night in January. The fire curtain was down, only the stalls were dimly lit, the upper tiers shrouded in darkness, the great chandelier invisible high up in the roof. Rambert, now rather frail, had to stand sandwiched between the front row of the stalls and the orchestra pit without a chair, a table or even a glass of water at her side. I felt she had been shabbily treated by the organisers. She had taken a lot of trouble with her appearance, looking extremely elegant in a full-length fur coat – which she needed– and her white hair beautifully coifed. Seemingly quite calm, even at that age she still had that extraordinary charisma that had carried her through her turbulent life. She would no doubt have been quite at home addressing a crowd of dockers, indeed, would have found them infinitely more interesting than this dull group of muted although quite self-opinionated followers of the ballet, mostly of the Royal Ballet. Undaunted, she gave a most inspiring talk standing for three-quarters of an hour. Her voice was now a shadow of its former raucousness, the voice of a frail old woman which did not reach the back of the stalls. Someone shouted 'Speak up!'

So a microphone was hastily rigged up while she stood patiently waiting leaning against the orchestra rail, no one offered her a chair.

She always spoke without notes, possessing a fantastic memory, she once told me that all her life she had memorised long poems late at night as an exercise for the brain. If she got stuck for a date she would implore the audience to prompt her and still recall it before them. She remembered composers, designers, choreographers with absolute accuracy, often lifting her head and closing her eyes in a characteristic gesture of concentration while she searched for the name of a dancer or composer. She had wonderful dramatic gestures which came quite naturally to her, the clasping of the hands and the lifting of the head in ecstasy as she recalled Nijinsky's final jump through the window of *Spectre de la Rose*, or the devastating finality of the movement of her hand as she dismissed some work as mediocre. I wondered how many in the audience actually understood all she told them. She gave a brilliant exposé of *Petrushka*, illuminating the characters of the dolls in a way that I had never fully understood even though I had danced many times in this ballet. The girl doll with her painted cheeks and eyelashes, embodying as Mim said all the stupidity of women, adoring the moronic Moor who worshipped a coconut, and being disgusted by the poor tortured Petrushka with the soul of a man and the body of a puppet. She ridiculed the people who had written so much nonsense about Nijinsky, saying that he was half-witted, and there was a roar of laughter from her by now fascinated audience when she quoted one writer who declared that when Nijinsky's feet were examined by a specialist this gentleman announced that he had the webbed feet of a bird and this explained the height of his jump. 'As if birds ever flew with their feet!' she quipped.

Although I was never officially invited to dinner, few were, I was occasionally offered a meal before driving us to the theatre. This took place in the small kitchen where the faithful Helen might have left an Irish stew keeping warm on the top of the old-fashioned gas stove, I doubt if anything new had been added to the kitchen since the 1930s. The dining-room was exactly as it had been in those far-off days when I had sat with the family over Marmite tea but it was seldom used. However, there was the rare occasion when Elisabeth Schooling was invited to dine. Mim ushered her into the dining room where the table was laid for two. Elisabeth sat down as bidden and Mim disappeared, after a long pause she returned empty handed. 'I'm so sorry', she said in a rather flustered voice, 'Helen is having one of her sulks and has not left us anything. Never mind', she said brightly, 'We will have bread and cheese.'

Norman Morrice joined the school for training in 1952 and would prove a valuable addition to the company when in 1958 he choreographed *Two Brothers*. Norman grew up in Mansfield, an industrial town in the Midlands where his father was an engineer. Norman fell in love with ballet when he saw a performance given by the then Sadler's Wells company in wartime. Robert Helpmann's ballet of *Hamlet* in particular fired his imagination and when later he saw Tudor's *Jardin aux lilas* in Nottingham he determined to become a choreographer.

There was a touch of *Billy Elliot* about his initial training in Mansfield. 'I was 19 and the only boy in a class of eight-year-old girls, but the teacher was a man which helped.' Both his parents were opposed to him becoming a dancer, he was studying science where he complained 'there were no mysteries', it was hardly a suitable subject for an imaginative young boy. He had a weedy physique and would never acquire a strong classical technique and failed his first audition for the Rambert School. He persevered with training and six months later auditioned again. He was put into Mim's class. 'She totally ignored me', he said and concluded she was not interested. After she'd left the studio he was called into the office where he was confronted by Erica Bowen whom he found quite alarming. To his surprise she announced in her grandest voice (kept especially for parents and new aspirants) 'Madame has accepted you'. Although at first she presented such an intimidating image, he was to be grateful to Erica once she took him under her wing and along with quite a few penniless students would take them back to her flat and feed them. 'However we did have to earn our bread by doing odd cleaning jobs about the flat, but that was only fair.'

He trained for a further two years, encouraged and helped by Mim. 'But the extraordinary thing was that having been so nice to me at school once I joined the company she turned into a monster! I thought she hated me. She made me pad my spindly legs and I had to wear enormous shoulder pads that came up to my ears, so of course I sweated so much I got even thinner!' He spent three boring years heavily disguised as the dollmaker Doctor Coppelius in the most popular ballet in the repertoire, *Coppélia*. During rehearsals the men had to learn all the girls' steps 'because she couldn't bear to see us idle'. Norman thought it was a good thing, that way he learnt all the repertoire.

Rambert was finding it difficult to find new choreographers of the calibre of Tudor and Ashton. She favoured Ronald Yerrell whom she thought had promise as a choreographer, but gave no encouragement to Norman. But he was determined to try and whenever possible during the exhausting touring schedule he persuaded some of the dancers to allow him to work out some of his ideas on them. Eventually he plucked up the courage to ask Mim to let him make an attempt at a ballet. Her response was to demand five minutes of composition and would only allow him to work with the dancers on two afternoons a week. When he was ready she called in Peter Williams, the dance critic, and one or two others to sound out their opinion of Norman's work. He passed the test and from then on she became an enthusiastic supporter. Mim warmed to him as a person and appreciated the fact that he was well educated, had a good mind and was quiet and thoughtful. Although she was always loyal to her dancers there were few of sufficient intellect to interest her.

By the latter end of the fifties things were looking up with a visit to Jacob's Pillow in the States, a week in Baalbek in the Lebanon and most fascinating of all a tour of China.

Towards the end of the fifties the company had regular work touring. A great asset was Lucette Aldous, a 'pocket ballerina'. She had been engaged by David Ellis when he became a director in 1955. It seems that although Lucette was a brilliant technical dancer with an engaging personality, she was not Rambert's type. Mim took no notice of her, gave her no encouragement and left it to Ellis to coach her in her roles. Perhaps because Lucette had been trained by Ninette de Valois Mim felt at a disadvantage, her own lack of early classical training haunted her. She gave Lucette quite a rough time even though Lucette in some respects saved Ballet Rambert. She became the Rambert ballerina, adding *Giselle*, *La Sylphide* and *Don Quixote* to her repertoire. There was no one else to match her in the company – but she was not 'a Rambert dancer'. In her memoir *Quicksilver*, Mim wrote, 'in our company the dancers all have the same status. They interchange parts and enrich every aspect of a role.' Perhaps that was the problem, Lucette felt herself a ballerina and expected to be given that status, but Rambert did not acknowledge this. Lucette was indignant when Mim told her not to book into hotels since the no.1 dressing room was furnished with a divan, wash-basin and dressing-table so Lucette should sleep there and save her money.

When on a trip to Australia in 1995 I watched Lucette teaching in Perth. I was intrigued to meet this tiny woman now well into middle-age. Still slim, she was fully made-up including long false eyelashes, wore tight-fitting practice clothes, and took the entire class on pointe. I had suggested that I give a talk to her students about the Ballet Club. Lucette was very cool at first but finally agreed. She sat stony-faced at the beginning of my talk but as I progressed her face softened and I even managed to extract a smile from her. She simply did not understand Mim and probably felt undervalued.

David having made a success of the Workshop was encouraged by Rambert to become involved in the company as her natural heir. Now in her sixties, she must have begun to find the constant touring wearying and uncomfortable, particularly in the winter months. She was delighted to be awarded the CBE in June 1954, and in 1957 received the Légion d'honneur. There would be several more honours over the next few years but the company that she had built up was in the fifties in grave danger of disappearing altogether. However, the company spirits were raised by an announcement in the newspaper about plans for the new theatre.

Ashley Dukes died in 1959 of a pulmonary embolism after taking his grandchildren on a boat ride on the Serpentine in Hyde Park. It was the first time in his life that he had been in hospital. Norman recalled the moment Rambert rushed in to make the announcement during the morning class. In spite of all the difficulties in their marriage Mim and Ashley were reconciled at the end. 'He had been the tree against which I grew', Mim said. Together they had made superhuman efforts to keep the company as an independent, family organisation, but from now on it would need outside help to keep going and Rambert herself, while receiving recognition and many awards for her contribution to the arts, would gradually loosen her hold and pass the mantle to successors.

CHAPTER 25

Through the fifties and sixties Rambert received the recognition for her work that brought her out of the shadows. This mattered to Mim, whereas de Valois preferred to keep in the background Mim needed attention to boost her frail self-confidence. De Valois, a visionary, always knew where she was going, Rambert did not.

In the coronation year of 1953 she was given a CBE, three years later the Queen Elizabeth II Coronation Award from the Royal Academy of Dancing, the Légion d'honneur from France in 1957. She was made a Dame Commander of the Order of the British Empire in 1962, a particular source of pride, although 'Ninette got there first', she quipped (de Valois had been made a Dame in 1951). Mim was also awarded a couple of Doctorates and a gold medal from the Polish Government in 1979. I visited Lulu in Tenerife in 1999. She hunted everywhere trying to find the medal to show me, to no avail. The following year she wrote to me, 'You'll never guess where I found it – in with the Christmas decorations!'

Although Mim must have been gratified by all this recognition she was never really satisfied. 'You know', she confided to me 'I have never known rich and influential people, not like Freddy who knows everyone, even the Duchess of Kent who is a great personal friend.' But this was not strictly true, Rambert was famous by now and had many admirers who appreciated her work and sought her company at dinner parties. Her correspondence was vast and she always answered her letters writing in longhand, a hand that trembled increasingly with the advance of age.

She had a wide circle of friends and admirers covering a broad spectrum of people either part of, or interested in, the arts; T.S. Eliot, Peggy Ashcroft, Diana Duff-Cooper (a personal friend), Alistair Cooke, Sybil Thorndike, Kenneth Clarke, and Isaiah Berlin (to whom she wrote in Russian). They all adored her. In 1971 she wrote to the Prime Minister recommending a knighthood for Peter Daubeny, the impresario who brought world theatre to the West End; she had a close friendship with Lincoln Kirstein, and Sacheverell Sitwell wrote to her in 1960, 'It is most important you continue your work for British ballet.'

She always answered her letters but if they were 'tiresome' passed them on to her secretary, such as the correspondence with Romola Nijinsky, 'I don't want anything to do with that awful woman', or Mabel Dolmetsch who ran the Historical Dance Society and had arranged the dances for *La Pomme d'or* in the early days of Rambert's career. In acknowledgement of her help Dame Marie at some time had become a patron of the Society. She must have pestered Rambert, perhaps for financial backing or expecting her to make personal appearances but Rambert had no time for her and protested that 'she wanted to be left in peace'. She instructed her secretary 'not to send her anything and have my name removed as soon as possible from headings'.

Rambert had progressed a long way away from her beginnings and particularly abhorred what she termed 'barefoot dancing' which presumably included her work with Dalcroze and her own recital work. Before the advent of Martha Graham and her company there were various organisations which called themselves modern dance. Pioneers of 'free' movement inspired by the German pre-war School of Mary Wigman, were no doubt doing useful work in Dance in Education but were not theatrically viable and frankly dated. The ballet profession tended to sneer at this kind of dancing and none more so than the fickle Mim herself. She would have to eat her words when her own company changed policy and threw off their shoes.

Apart from teaching classical and character dance at the school I also took over Lulu's modern class. I was aware that my knowledge of what was now called contemporary dance was limited and I invited Anne Woolliams who was teaching at the Folkwang School in Essen (by now the Kurt Jooss headquarters) to watch one of my classes. She told me that Robert Cohan from the Martha Graham company was giving a summer course at the school and invited me. Despite having no money and with no encouragement or financial backing from Angela I packed my bags and went – steerage. By now over forty, I tortured my poor stiff body for three gruelling weeks, burning the midnight oil, making copious notes and diagrams in my notebook, fascinated by the Graham technique and by Cohan the Guru. It was my last love affair with dance, born at a different time I might well have become a modern dancer.

On my return, aflame with enthusiasm I met Rambert in the dressing-room. 'Oh Breegee! where have you been?' she said. She half listened to my glowing account of the course but the moment I said 'Martha Graham' she pulled a face and shrieked 'Oh! Martha Graham! Barefoot dancing!' and flounced out of the room. I was shattered. What an extraordinary woman! She had seen the Graham company in 1954 when they came to the Saville theatre and in her own memoir she writes, 'I was completely carried away, both by her choreography and by her impeccable dancing in her own idiom.' Her reaction to my studying the technique was incomprehensible but of course she was totally unpredictable. Perhaps she simply did not like my enthusiasm for Graham, perhaps it was personal. Undeterred, I continued to study with the Graham dancers, returning to Germany to work with Yoriko, Mary Hinkson, Ethel Winter and taking classes up at The Place. I tore around attending lecture demonstrations at the American Embassy and watching performances. Robin Howard towards whom I felt a great regard and affection persuaded Angela to stage a lecture-dem at the Mercury. Rambert was not in evidence but Martha herself came and gave an inspiring talk to the students. I have no idea what thoughts raced through Angela's head, but both she and eventually Mim herself saw which way the wind was blowing and sailed along with it.

I pride myself on having given a helping hand to promote Contemporary Dance before it had been accepted by the mainstream of ballet. When the Rambert School in the seventies was seeking premises to continue its existence I went to see Robin Howard. He was a charming, sincere man who bravely went about his daily involvement with his new Contemporary Dance Centre, The Place, up in Euston despite the fact that he had lost both legs in a tank explosion on the last day of the war. On this particular visit to his house he took me down in the lift to his private office. I was surprised to see a large photograph of Rambert over his desk. 'You're very privileged, I don't bring many people down here. I adored her,' he said.

Afterwards when we were back upstairs in the official reception area Robin said quietly, 'It's strange how the Rambert organisation has a long history of disloyalty to the very people who have worked so hard to promote it.' He seemed to think that I had not been well treated – even Rambert herself had told me that I was 'too modest' at one point. Howard was an idealist who did not really know much about the profession he had so wholeheartedly espoused, or indeed those who ran it. He gave almost every penny he had to the promotion of an art he adored. Ironically he was treated just as shabbily by his own board of directors and was booted out. An innocent who had braved the jungle of English dance, he believed that because dancers were beautiful in movement they had beautiful souls.

In 1957 the Rambert company had toured China, the first British company to do so. It was extraordinary that this company, for ever in danger of extinction, crashing on from one financial crisis to another should nevertheless from time to time be performing in unusual situations, pioneering and paving the way for subsequent more secure companies.

Mim's letters home were fascinating, written in pencil on scruffy little pages torn out of a cheap notepad or even on cheap toilet paper. Whether this was yet another example of her parsimony or simply all that was available, they make amusing reading. She paid a visit to Russia on her way to China and boasted that she had walked for twelve hours in Moscow and slept on the plane to China so heavily (thanks to Bell's Miracle Pills) that the crew became worried. They tried to wake her but without success, so they called a doctor. 'She shook me hard and when I opened my eyes and saw her taking my pulse I laughed heartily and went back to sleep again.'

She wrote that 'Peking was wonderful; lovely stage, palatial dressing-rooms with rugs fit for our drawing-room, gorgeous huge classrooms (floor very slippery) but hideous spittoons in all the rooms!'

In 1959 they performed at Jacob's Pillow in the USA and on their return journey in Baalbek, 'against those fabulous ruins', as Rambert put it.

In 1966 the policy of the Rambert company changed direction. The classical repertoire was jettisoned, including some of the most interesting and seminal works of Ashton, Howard and Tudor, many of which were never performed again. What must Mim have felt when this dramatic decision was taken? Did she fight for her Ballet Club oeuvres, for that's what they were? It is a paradox that in spite of that fiery temperament, those noisy tantrums, her capacity for fighting for perfection in her teaching, Rambert never seems to have found the courage to fight for what must have been so dear to her heart, those unique little ballets that had won such acclaim in so many parts of the world and that had made her name. But had she not said many years before, 'I am a coward'? So there it was, Ballet Rambert became a 'contemporary troupe', as one dance magazine put it. One can only suppose that Mim had been advised that this was an avant garde evolution, and wasn't that what she and Ashley had always stood for? Christopher Bruce was to say later in 2001, 'I think that's what Rambert would have wished, because the future of this company lies in its creativity'.

Norman Morrice, a gentle man, was charged with the delicate mission of informing David Ellis that he would no longer be artistic director. Norman was invited to lunch, he was a brave man. David and Angela, one presumes, expected a 'meeting of minds' to discuss the future of the company. Instead Norman, as tactfully as he could, explained that he had been offered the directorship of the company under the new policy. He had agreed on condition that David stepped down. To his astonishment Angela took it quite coolly and told David, 'It was about time that someone said that!' This probably referred to the fact that her husband was forever touring and she wanted him back home.

In 1972 Rambert's autobiography *Quicksilver* was published. She had been reluctant to write it as she proved when one evening in the stalls at Covent Garden I asked her why she was not writing her memoirs. There was a pause, then she replied crisply; 'It would have to be called "Here lies Marie Rambert". No, I am not a writer', and dismissed the subject.

She was of course helped in the writing and one of the helpers, Vera Chapman wrote, 'It doesn't seem like five years ago that you and I struggled with the final typing of your manuscript. I also recall the last time I came to your house with the last chapters, when you were ill, and you said to me, "I don't suppose anyone will want to read it!" And then, when Macmillans asked you to fill it out a bit, you felt you had had enough and would not be able to face going through it all again, you said to me, "I shall probably put your beautifully typed pages away and then perhaps some day my daughter will write it for me."' Mim wrote a message to her secretary about the letter, 'Keep this, it is absolutely correct and I had forgotten.' The instruction was to ring Mrs Chapman and send her a signed copy, the same was done to all of Mim's friends – in the end she was proud of her book.

* * * * *

8.55 am on a February morning in 1962. The double entrance doors to the Mercury were thrown wide open to the bitter cold outside. The teachers and pianists stood shivering with cold in the draughty foyer awaiting the arrival of Rambert for her 9 o'clock class. A television van was parked outside from which long cables like the entrails of a dinosaur wound over the pavement, up the steps, through the open doors and into the foyer.

A large avuncular man with a big face stood holding a large book and looking expectantly towards the open doors. Behind him crouched as unobtrusively as possible the camera crew. Erica fussed around in a terrible state,

'I'm *so* sorry, Madame is *never* late as a rule.'

The big man smiled indulgently and in a strong Irish brogue told her not to worry. Mim finally arrived looking awful and very cross. She was wearing a shabby dung-coloured coat, baggy black trousers, her head muffled up in a colourless shawl against the biting wind. We stood silently watching her mounting the steps, weaving her way through the yards of cable, bewildered to see so many people standing around so early in the morning. She glared at us, we stirred uncomfortably, was she going to stage one of her temperaments?

'What is all this all over the place?' she said, crossly indicating the cables – then looking up at the big man advancing towards her wreathed in smiles she added 'And who are you? You're very tall, what are you doing here?' Whereupon Eamonn Andrews presented her with the album and uttered the immortal words: 'Dame Marie Rambert, this is your life!'

'Oh no!' she shrieked in an agonised voice. A shade of annoyance crossed her features. Then suddenly aware that the cameras were running, true 'pro' that she was, she switched on the benign smile of the fairy godmother, received the album graciously in her two hands and performed her *Grand Révérence* to Andrews who was of course overwhelmed at the honour.

CHAPTER 26

It is debatable how far into old age a ballet teacher should carry on giving classes. The three famous Russian teachers in Paris, Olga Preobrajenska, Lubov Egorova and Mathilde Kchessinska taught well into advanced old age and I saw on a visit to the Vaganova school in St Petersburg some of the teachers were very old indeed, sometimes crippled with arthritis . But then they all had to earn their living. This was not so with Mim, she carried on simply because she loved it.

Ninette de Valois said that a teacher should retire at sixty which seemed, as with many of her edicts, a little harsh, but then she was not talking about the great independent teachers who ran their own studios. A teacher who can no longer demonstrate will have a favourite pupil who will do this for her (or him), acting as the maestro's *aide memoire* when if comes to setting adagios and enchainements. Such was the case with Nicholas Legat. This was not the case in Mim's classes, she expected the students to immediately memorise her enchainements even when she forgot them herself and she became confused and irritated when she got lost. She kept the dancers for far too long on the barre, probably because she could still keep control. The students became increasingly frustrated by the pauses when Mim changed her mind, standing about getting cold.

It couldn't go on, something had to be done to convince her to retire from teaching. Now well into her eighties there had been a suggestion of minor heart or perhaps blood-pressure trouble from her doctor, not serious, but enough for Angela and David to be able to convince her to give up. Mim was not pleased but she eventually bowed out much to the relief of both students and staff. Still, they missed her presence especially as she now distanced herself from the school.

Occasionally she was called upon to put in an appearance and would pop in to watch my character class which she enjoyed. I relished her witty comments. 'What is this gesture they are making, Breegee?', she enquired of a Russian dance. 'They're distributing grain, Madame', I explained. 'Or propaganda leaflets', she quipped. She put her nose round the studio door one afternoon when I was teaching a very crowded class which included two unusually tall girls. 'What a *huge* class, and *what* huge girls', she

commented and disappeared. She did not enjoy coming to the school now that she felt it was no longer *her* school.

She sometimes invited me to accompany her to a performance when I would pick her up at the house and drive her. On one such occasion in the sixties I was invited to supper prior to taking her to the theatre. I was ushered into the small kitchen and bidden to sit down at a card table covered with a cloth and laid for the two of us. I doubt if much had changed since the early days of the family, the decoration was drab and there was a general air of seediness. A faint whiff of wet dishcloths hung about the place and the cracked old lino was none too clean.

Helen had left a stew in a saucepan on the elderly gas stove. Mim grabbed the saucepan and shovelled a rather grey mixture onto my plate and bade me eat it all up. It wasn't too bad, and I would not have dared leave anything on my plate. However, the fruit bowl was impressive and I was glad to fill up on an apple.

Although Mim was extravagant in her praise of her devoted housekeeper she kept her so short of money that Helen sometimes resorted to desperate measures, the paucity of her housekeeping money taxed her ingenuity in providing meals and general necessities. Mim did not encourage luxuries in what she ate nor would she allow Helen to buy flowers or indeed any unnecessary ornamentation about the house. Frustrated, Helen would appropriate plants from neighbouring window boxes, and more seriously, titbits from Marks & Spencers. When Helen died Mim was quite shattered. 'She was a wonderful woman.'

Tamara Finch, the former Tamara Tchinarova, paid Rambert a visit and on arrival presented her with a big bunch of flowers. Mim frowned and commented that she would have preferred some fruit. Tamara gasped at such rudeness.

Mim, contrary to some people's opinion, had great humility towards the arts and towards religion. She believed in the 'will of God'. This became paramount in her attitude to life, her religion supported and aided her toward acceptance of old age. She attended Mass regularly in the Carmelite Church in Kensington. The nuns were her friends, and her Irish maids, particularly the faithful Helen, had exerted a strong influence on her. She had been a devout Catholic all her life although it is uncertain when she became converted. Aged 92 and contemplating her death she became anxious about her religion. Born Jewish, she was concerned about the possibility of going to purgatory. She wrote a letter to the Carmelite sisters seeking comfort in their wisdom.

She now had the leisure to enjoy her five grandchildren in a way that had been impossible with her two daughters. She had finally given up turning cartwheels once she became a Dame, considering it 'unsuitable'. At one point she took up typing, she could not stand idleness. She was lonely, there was no doubt about that, but when they got her a paid companion Rambert hated her and no doubt the poor woman was not too sorry to be dismissed. The bright black boot-button eyes were now hooded by drooping eyelids but every now and then they flashed like electric sparks at the remembrance of something which had annoyed her and she still relished a fiendish attack on the shortcomings of a previous student or person encountered in her past life. Still quite upright she did not use a stick, her sight seemed to be good. I never saw her wear spectacles and although probably her hearing was slightly impaired she never let on. There did not seem to be any rheumatic problems and no arthritis, that scourge of the dancer, but then she had not taxed her body overmuch, she was the torturer not the tortured. However, her misshapen shoes bore testimony to her struggles to achieve an arch but she seemed to have no difficulty with walking and went to Holland Park every day.

Norman lived in the basement flat in the house and became a personal friend to Rambert in her old age and often accompanied her on her walks. In her final years he would visit her in her bedroom, during the winter months wearing his overcoat, 'It was freezing!' They never talked about ballet, it was something you did, not talked about. Their talks were more likely to have been about literature, drama. 'I still miss this woman, she had such a lust for art', Norman said after she died.

When John Tooley approached Norman with the offer to become Director of the Royal Ballet, Norman hesitated, he would be the first outsider to take up such a position with the Royal Ballet and felt daunted by the contemplation of such an onerous responsibility, but Rambert said, 'Darling, it is your duty to accept. We must talk to Ninette', and invited her to tea. When Norman appeared the two Dames were so deeply engrossed in their conversation that the purpose of his visit was totally forgotten and Norman returned to his damp basement having got no further. He was fascinated to meet this rather intimidating woman with 'haunted eyes which sized up people and situations with extraordinary accuracy'.

One evening, when Rambert was ninety, I rang intending to make an appointment to pay her a visit. Her frail little voice expressed bewilderment. 'Next week? How do you know I shall still be here? Come now.'

Helen opened the door and took me up to her bedroom. A radio, a small television, the phone and numerous books formed a cosy circle in the midst of which lay, propped up by numerous pillows, a little bird in a pink nightie. I'd brought her some flowers.

'Oh no, you shouldn't spend your money', she said disapprovingly, then when I told her they were roses from my garden she said 'Oh, that's different.' I glanced around the room looking for a wastepaper basket in which to throw the wrapping.

'I'm not allowed a waste-paper basket', she said like a mischievous child. I wondered why. 'Aren't I lucky, I have everything I need all around me. Have you seen my medals?' I shook my head. 'They're in the drawer of that cabinet, bring them over.' She showed them to me with great pride, 'Aren't they beautiful?' I felt very privileged. 'Now put them back.' I obeyed like the obedient child which I had always been in her eyes.

'Sit down, there', she ordered, indicating a chair at the foot of the bed. 'Take your shoes off and put your feet under the eiderdown, I know how tired one is at the end of a teaching day.'

'Do you invite everyone who visits you to do this?' I enquired.

'No – only Kelly.'

'What does it feel like to be ninety?'

'Awful, I have no more interest in life, I just want to die', she said brightly.

'Now tell me about your visit to Poland.'

And with intense interest she made me recount every detail of my recent visit. What performances had I seen? I told her about the unusual *Twelfth Night* I had seen in which the cast were all women. She spoke about Tudor's first work, *Cross Garter'd*.

'He wanted to choreograph after only six months' training. I made him show me one dance which convinced me he had talent.'

I asked how she spent her day – she still did her barre which she spelt out like a menu: 'Two *pliés* in second, two in first... then *tendues* and so on.'

The Rambert School closed its doors in 1979, the Mercury was sold to a property developer and the school moved in temporarily with the London School of Contemporary Dance at The Place in Euston. It was a most distressing time for everybody who loved the Mercury, and for myself having known it since I was twelve years old, it was a shock. Rambert and my mother were the greatest influences in my life and I felt I was losing my home. In my bewilderment I must have written to Mim hoping perhaps for an explanation as to what had happened and seeking her guidance. She sent me a card with the famous photograph of herself as a child on which she wrote:

Darling Briggy 14.7.80

I was so touched by your words, thank you a thousand times. Somehow the situation is too difficult to explain... No explanation would enlighten you or justify me – but it had to be thus.

Much, much love

Mim

I went to see her, expecting as before to find her in bed but she was in the drawing-room all in pink again, warm dressing-gown, socks, slippers, pink cheeks to match, snowy white hair and a bright smile. As I entered through the door Mim, using the mantlepiece as a barre, demonstrated the ghost of an adage, moving her head and her arm beautifully, standing perilously on one leg in a low arabesque, a blissful expression on her face. She wanted to show me she could still do it.

She took my hand in her little thin one, led me over to the sofa, sat me down and continued holding my hand while questioning me on the latest news. I'd never seen this side of Mim, warm and loving. In spite of her great age – she was ninety-three by then – she was still perfectly coherent, forgetting a name occasionally, getting her dates mixed, but the black eyes, dimmed beneath the drooping lids, were as piercing as ever. She who had shouted louder than anyone now frowned when I raised my voice and pleaded, 'Shush! Quietly, quietly.'

She told me that Dame Ninette visited her frequently and it was plain that the old rivalries had faded into the past.

'You know, that is a remarkable woman, she is so modest, she doesn't seem to realise what a wonderful thing she did in founding the Royal Ballet. She has no conceit whatsoever and she is so intelligent, so knowledgeable.'

I was struck by the humility of this woman who herself had made such an enormous contribution to English ballet.

Rambert died in June 1982. She had two strokes, the second one fatal. She did not have to endure a long illness, in fact she was in good health right to the end – it was all over in 24 hours.

At Rambert's funeral service (in 1982) de Valois returned the compliment.

'Marie Rambert had that unusual attribute – intelligence and intellectualism – a rare combination.'

It fell to me to announce Mim's death to the students at the The Place. I fought back the tears, aware that this new breed of Rambert student never knew her. They watched me struggling to find adequate words but I realised that although they were listening politely, for them Rambert had already become just a name in history. Mim would not have had it otherwise.

EPILOGUE

Angela phoned me one day in the eighties, 'We've sold the Mercury – I thought you might want to pay it a last visit.' I went along with my camera and wandered through the studios, nodding at the ghastly old boiler, stroking the same old barres, shivering at the draughts thrusting through the ill-fitting skylight. One early morning in midwinter there had been a heavy downfall of snow, Angela clad in nightdress, her shower cap and raincoat, had to shovel away a large mound of snow that had entered through the skylight and dumped itself in the old studio.

The theatre studio was gloomy, the famous little stage now cluttered with old pieces of wood and canvas, props and general litter, the dismal scene rendered even darker by the black paintwork on the brick walls, left over from the last production of a small dramatic group that had hired the theatre. There was no sentimentality and Angela did not express any regret, her practical nature had accepted the situation and indeed was probably thankful to get rid of what had become a heavy burden. The tree that stood right opposite the stage door fell onto the roof during the great gale. It seemed prophetic.

Myself? I don't recall being particularly moved, only angry that the theatre could not have been preserved for future generations of ballet people as a museum or a library. Angela said she had approached one or two rich patrons but no one showed any interest. It was a valuable site and was sold at the height of a property boom .

In the late seventies the Rambert School was still thriving, so that when Angela Ellis suddenly announced its closure it came as a great shock to both students and staff. It was a shock to myself although by that time I was dividing my time between teaching actors at LAMDA and at the Rambert School.

In retrospect it was obvious that there were logical reasons for the decision to close this famous, historic school; the age of its directors and many of the staff, Angela herself was now sixty; Rambert was no longer in evidence; and most importantly the increasingly dilapidated state of the building.

When in the sixties the CDET (Council for Dance Education and Training) was founded certain criteria were set where not only the standard of the teaching but also the suitability of premises had to be an acceptable standard in order for students to receive grants. A list of approved schools was issued for the guidance of local authorities. To Angela's fury, the Rambert School was not on that list since there had been no inspection, the door having been securely closed in the face of the CDET. The building needed huge sums of money to be spent on modernisation. Angela had had enough and, it could be said, the arrogance of the family in refusing to fall in with current developments antagonised the CDET. In the event the Rambert School was added to the list but with probably a warning that while not questioning the high standard of the training, sooner or later the premises would have to be inspected, and changed.

In the new age of comfort, facilities and amenities had priority over the artistic values. Here was this crumbling old church hall crammed with happy, hard-working, eager young folk willing to put up with discomfort for the sake of pursuing their ambitions to 'get out there' and earn their living in their chosen profession. Never mind that there were only two lavatories, no showers, no canteen, no staffroom, potentially lethal electric wires dangling from the walls, leaky pipes and no central heating. The young people loved the place for its very eccentricity, they always had done for generations of dancers.

After much heated wrangling the school was put on the list but the Ellises, true to the tradition of not extending the begging bowl to pay for modernisation, made the decision to close the school down and take up Robin Howard's offer to temporarily house the school at The Place while a new home was sought. After four years working quite happily there the school finally amalgamated with the Rambert Academy in Isleworth.

What were Mim's feelings about losing her former nest? Since she was no longer part of it, having passed the school to Angela, she had distanced herself from it for some time and showed little interest. In one way she felt cheated of her heritage, there was some bitterness, but her heart lay with her company, she was realistic enough to see where her loyalties lay.

INDEX

Lightning Source UK Ltd.
Milton Keynes UK
24 November 2009

146663UK00001B/99/P